MRS. FRANCES HOPPE AND HER SON WILLIE PLAYING
A BILLIARDS MATCH, 1900

This photograph by Byron is from the Byron Collection of the Museum of the
City of New York.

# THIRTY YEARS OF BILLIARDS

BY

## WILLIE HOPPE

EDITED BY

**THOMAS EMMETT CROZIER**

DOVER PUBLICATIONS, INC.
NEW YORK

Published in Canada by General Publishing Company, Ltd., 30 Lesmill Road, Don Mills, Toronto,
Ontario.
Published in the United Kingdom by Constable
and Company, Ltd., 10 Orange Street, London WC 2.


This Dover edition, first published in 1975, is an
unabridged republication of the work originally
published by G. P. Putnam's Sons, New York, in
1925. A new Publisher's Note has been added to the
present edition.


International Standard Book Number: 0-486-23126-7
Library of Congress Catalog Card Number: 74-15003

Manufactured in the United States of America
Dover Publications, Inc.
180 Varick Street
New York, N.Y. 10014

# NOTE TO THE DOVER REPRINT

WILLIE HOPPE published this autobiography, *Thirty Years of Billiards,* in 1925, when he was thirty-eight years old. It chronicles the years during which he toured as a child prodigy, won the 18.1 balk-line championship from Maurice Vignaux of France, and went on to become the world's greatest player of 18.2 balk-line billiards. Balkline billiards is not a familiar game today, and the reader who has never played it may want a word of explanation.

In 18.1 balk-line billiards, lines are drawn on the billiard table 18 inches from the rails along all four sides of the table. These lines, parallel to the sides of the table, intersect at four points and thus divide the billiard table into nine spaces, eight around the sides and one in the middle. If at any time both object balls come to rest within any one of the eight "balk spaces" around the sides of the table, the balls are then "in balk" and the player is obligated to make at least one of them leave that balk space on his next shot. A ball that is touching a line is in balk. If both balls are touching the same line, the player can decide which balk space they are considered to be in. The moved ball may return to the same balk space on that shot but it must at any rate cross at least one line first. While both object balls are in the middle space, the player may score as many points as he is able to without being obligated to first drive either of the object balls across a line. In 18.2 balk-line billiards, the player must drive at least one of the object balls across a line no later than on the second shot after the balls are in balk. It was in the game 18.2 balk-line billiards that Hoppe scored most of the victories recounted in this book. Basic billiard techniques are, however, common to all billiard games, and readers today will find Hoppe's thirty-six billiard lessons at the end of this book as useful as did the balk-line player of fifty years ago.

In the decade after the first publication of this book, balk-line billiards was replaced as the game of the great billiard champions by the modern three-cushion game, and Hoppe's extraordinary career entered its second phase. Taking up the modern game, he won his first three-cushion title in 1936. In the Chicago world tournament of 1940,

Hoppe scored his greatest victory, winning the championship by taking twenty straight games, a new record for tournament play. After 1940 Hoppe won the three-cushion title seven times; his last championship came in San Francisco in 1952, after which he retired from tournament play. He died at age seventy-one of a heart attack in Miami on February 1, 1959.

# CONTENTS

# ILLUSTRATIONS

# Thirty Years of Billiards

MR. HOPPE PLAYS AS WELL IN SOUP AND FISH AS
IN A JERSEY JACKET

This is his playing costume for an exhibition at the Union
League Club—or the White House.

# Thirty Years of Billiards

## CHAPTER I

### I STAND UPON A CHAIR AND MAKE SOME EXPERIMENTS WITH A CUE

My father was a barber.  Early in the eighteen nineties he rented the ground floor of a little brick hotel at Cornwall Landing, fifty-three miles north of New York City on the west bank of the Hudson. In half of it he set up a lunch room and in the other half, with a wooden partition between, a barber shop.

My mother took charge of the lunch room, serving home-cooked meals to hungry railroad men, barge hands and miscellaneous travellers, while my father bossed the shop.

It was more than a barber shop.  It was the social center of our little town.  When the trains from the city had come and gone, hack-drivers and drummers used to gather there to warm their hands at the big iron stove and talk about the weather.  Besides the stove and the two red plush barber chairs the shop boasted a battle-scarred old billiard table.

I was born October 11, 1887 and some of my earliest recollections are centered around that billiard table. I can remember standing beside the stove watching the bright-colored balls rolling helter-skelter across the green cloth, bouncing off the cushions, colliding, disappearing suddenly and unexpectedly with a "plop!" in the pockets that yawned at the corners.

At the age of five or six I first got on a friendly footing with the billiard table and its mysteries. My brother Frank, who was two years older and several inches taller than I, already was permitted to rack up the balls and retrieve them from the pockets. When a game was finished he used to pick up a cue and walk around the table with a superior air, poking at the balls and making a great clatter, while I, standing on tiptoe with my nose just above the rail, watched the performance with awe and admiration.

One day my father lifted me up on a chair, placed a cue in my hands and arranged two balls near a corner pocket. He told me how to hold the cue so it would slide easily through the fingers of my left hand, how to aim at the first ball and where to hit the second. Two or three hack-drivers gathered around to watch the fun, while Frank looked on with critical eye. I lunged out bravely, and missed it a mile. Frank snickered. More than thirty years have passed, but I think I can still hear the echo of his chuckle at my first mis-cue.

I tried it again, and again I missed; but the third time I was rewarded by seeing the object ball roll to the corner, wobble a bit uncertainly, and then disappear. That was the thrill that comes once in a life-time. After that, it wasn't long before I was marching around the table with Frank, matching him stroke for stroke in the pocket game.

The table was much too high for me. There were only a few shots I could reach on tip-toe from the floor. So my Grandfather Hoffman made a little wooden bench for me to stand on. But there were some shots I could not reach, even from the bench. For these I would climb up on the table and lie at full length, with my heels up among the kerosene lamps that hung over head.

Carrying my wooden platform from one side of the table to the other, stretching my arms at all angles, lying "belly-whopper" on the table bed, I soon was on familiar terms with the old table and its mysteries.

My stroke developed in a peculiar way; because I was so short I had to hold my cue at the side of my head with my right hand. Consequently my fore-arm and wrist did most of the work, and the elevation of the cue was greater than if I had used the

orthodox under-arm swing from the shoulder.  But
that side-arm stroke has been one of the most valuable assets of my billiard career.  It has enabled me
to put a greater degree of twist, or "English" on the
ball with a softer stroke, than the ordinary method.
In close position play, too, it puts action on the ball
with a very delicate touch.

While my shortness of stature was a serious hand-
icap in getting about the table, it was an advantage
in another direction.  With my head just barely
projecting above the top of the table, my eyes were
down on a level with the line of play.  When I took
aim across the top of the cue ball I could measure
the angle much more accurately than if my head had
been in the normal position.

In the winter, the billiard table was a playground
for Frank and me.  When school was out and our
chores were done, we would hurry to the barber
shop.  To add to the natural rivalry between us,
there was always a group of hack-drivers, barbers
and travelling salesmen to spur us on.  Sometimes
the barbers were busy; sometimes there were no
drummers, but the hack-drivers were always there.
They could be depended on for advice, appreciation
and applause at all hours of the day and well into
the night.

How those old characters linger in my memory!
Jim Lewis owned the village livery stable and drove

one of his own hacks. He was the village fat man.
He didn't play much of a game of billiards; in fact
he had difficulty getting close enough to the table
to play at all. But he was a great match-maker.
He would put up ten cents or a quarter for Frank
and me to play for, and then referee the game.

Johnny Hall, another hack-driver, was the best
player in Cornwall. They called him "Seventeen
Cent Johnny" because on a certain occasion when
he tried to get in a card game with the other drivers
they made him show his bank roll, and all he could
produce, after exploring all his pockets, was 17
cents.

Johnny would play both of us together, and he
beat us easily at first. But we worked out a system
that finally turned the tables on him. I would shoot
first. Instead of trying to pocket any of the balls
I would whale into them with all my might, leaving
them spread all over the table. Then Frank, shooting next, would pocket as many as he could and then
leave Johnny safe.

We worked that same system against many other
experts that came to town. By the time I was 8
years old we had conquered the champions of Newburgh and Poughkeepsie by our team play.

Visiting drummers were our best customers, however, and the hack-drivers took keen delight in
steering them our way. If they saw a lonely sales-

man waiting around the station for his train they would approach him something like this:

"Stranger, do you play billiards? They've a table over in the Commercial barber shop and a couple of youngsters 8 or 9 years old that play quite a game. Why don't you go over and take them on?"

His curiosity aroused, the drummer would wander over to the barber shop and the hack-drivers would flock in after him to watch the fun. Frank would engineer the preliminaries, making the game, while I racked up the balls. There was always a little diplomatic maneuvering before the encounter began. Then "bang!" and the game was on. Many a salesman missed his train trying to beat Frank and me at our own game and many a dime went into our little tin bank as a result of these encounters.

Up to this time my father had regarded our playing as a mixed blessing. We were always under foot in the barber shop; always clambering around the table when somebody else wanted to play. But on the other hand we were attracting business to the shop and our skill with the cue was causing quite a bit of comment up and down the West Shore.

Finally, in the Spring of 1895 my father began to see financial possibilities in our talent. If we could clean up the home talent around Cornwall Landing and astonish the native sons with our amazing shots, why not clean up the talent of Kingston,

"WE HAD SOME LITTLE HAND BILLS PRINTED . . . AND FARED
FORTH TO ASTONISH THE WORLD"

Willie Hoppe (right) and his brother Frank, at 7 and 9, were earning the family
living with their cues.

Albany, Syracuse, Buffalo; and indeed, why not astonish the world?

We had some little hand bills printed:

HOPPE BROTHERS

THE BOY BILLIARDISTS

And away we started!

# CHAPTER II

## WE TOUR THE BUSH LEAGUE BILLIARD ROOMS AND
## LEARN SOMETHING OF LIFE

MY father made arrangements for Frank and me to play an exhibition at Kingston, N. Y., in February, 1895. That was our first engagement on a tour that was to take us through New York State.

My mother bade us a tearful farewell at the door, and the hack-drivers were out in force to give us a hilarious send-off at the station. We stopped in Newburgh to have our photograph taken, each holding his private cue in his right hand, with an ivory cue ball in his left.

I can't recall a trace of stage-fright as we stepped to the table at Kingston that night to play our first match in public. By this time we were thoroughly at home at the billiard table, and we were keen to show our wares to the skeptical strangers up the Hudson. The first exhibition netted ten dollars— enough to foot the hotel bill, pay our fares to Albany, and leave a small margin in reserve.

An old scrap-book records that we played Charles Hazen at Albany, Seth Hendricks at Troy, Frederick Doyle at Albion, Hannibal Jones at Middletown, Henry Clew at Rochester and Charlie Simons at Buffalo. Of these old-time players I remember little. But on that first trip, two or three things made a very distinct impression on my young mind.

My father was no longer the tolerant, easy-going parent of the Cornwall Landing barber shop days. He took our playing a great deal more seriously, now. He used to sit at the edge of the table during a match, watching every shot like a hawk. He would coach us in German, saying "Nein! nein!" in a sharp whisper if we chose the wrong shot. Nearly every miss brought a torrent of vigorous German swear-words, of which "Gott in Himmel" and "Dunder und Blitzen" were the mildest.

He was very strict and stern about our practice sessions, too. A capable player, himself, he knew how every shot on the table should be executed, and he expected nothing short of perfection from us. Hour after hour, chiefly in the mornings, he would have us at the table, drilling us in long cut shots, break shots and cross-table banks. And more than once, when we were dull or slow, he would give us a sound box on the ears.

Occasionally we would strike a town where my

father couldn't make a deal for an exhibition. Very well, if they wouldn't give us a chance to play in public, we'd find another way to make expenses. Frank and I would sit quietly by the wall in a strange billiard room, where we were unknown, while my father would engage one of the local experts in a game. He could beat most of them. By and by he would make some caustic comment.

"Where did you ever get the idea you could play pocket billiards?" he would say. "Why, I've got a nine-year-old boy there that can beat you."

And if the stranger showed any belligerent signs, my father would arrange a game with Frank, and Frank would proceed to trim him.

In our exhibition matches, my father would back us for various small amounts if the local players thought they had a chance. Sometimes we would lose, and then my father's moods were darkest. His stern lectures in German were greatly enjoyed by the spectators, but poor Frank, who received the major portion of the blame when we lost a game. took them very much to heart.

When things were going well; when either of us would clean all 15 balls off the table, my father would pat us on the shoulder and say, "Das ist gut," and "Gut Kind."

We had a wide variety of opponents. I remember one man, a tall, dark, sombre fellow who wore spectacles, who was determined to beat us. He mumbled to himself while he was shooting, and tried various ways to distract our attention.

He sat near the end of the table, and whenever Frank or I would try a corner pocket shot, he would light a cigarette, so that the flare of the match would take our eye off the ball. Some of his friends, sitting around the table joined with him in the little conspiracy, and every time we would try a difficult shot a match would be struck somewhere around the ring of spectators, to annoy us.

My father was furious. If we had lost that game, there might have been disastrous consequences. But we pulled through by a narrow margin.

Those dim, smoky rooms were not the most pleasant places in the world for two youngsters, not yet ten years old, but Frank and I got a lot of fun out of it. And when we returned to Cornwall, we had great tales to tell our mother, and the hack-drivers, about the conquests we had made up the river.

My recollection is that we made just a little more than expenses on that first trip in February and March, 1895. But my father had big ideas. He was sure the public would be willing to pay generously to see his two youngsters perform if he could take us on a tour of the great cities.

That summer we practised daily, and perfected our strokes, still under our father's exacting eye,

and early in the Fall he made a trip down the river
to New York City.   Back he came in a day or two
with big news.

Maurice Daly, the former champion billiard
player, and owner of two big parlors in New York
had engaged us to play a series of exhibitions at his
rooms in Brooklyn.   At last we were about to break
into the Big League.

# CHAPTER III

## WE PLAY FOR MAURICE DALY IN BROOKLYN, AND I
### RECEIVE SOME SOUND ADVICE

THE news that Frank and I were going to New
York City to play a series of exhibition matches in
one of the great billiard rooms caused quite a furore
around Cornwall Landing. We spread the news
among our school mates up in the village, and they,
too, became quite excited about it.

For more than a week prior to that eventful
Monday my brother and I practised diligently and
the old billiard table in the barber shop resounded
to the click of flying balls. We rehearsed bank
shots, combinations and freak formations while our
friends the barbers and hack-drivers looked on and
offered advice.

My mother was not yet reconciled to the idea of
our venturing out in the world at such a tender age.
But when the great day came, she dressed us in our
best blouses, tied our bow ties and sent us away

bravely, with as much cheerfulness as she could muster.

My father went with us, of course; and again, as the West Shore train pulled out, the station platform was lined with hack-drivers, waving their whips, and shouting friendly messages.

We carried our own private cues and each of us, in our trousers pocket, had a trusty piece of chalk. We might have depended on Mr. Daly to provide these small essentials, but on such a great occasion we were not in any mood to take chances.

West Point . . . Haverstraw . . . Weehawken! A marvelous ride on a ferry-boat across the river; electric cars; a great deal of noise and confusion, with my father pointing out the car window, "This is Broadway." "Yonder is Madison Square Garden," "Daly's Theatre" and "The Old Astor House."

We were completely bewildered by the time we reached the billiard room on Washington Street, Brooklyn; yet new wonders were in store for us. What an extraordinary establishment it was! Gas lights, a great mahogany bar across one wall, a carpet on the floor and as many as eighteen billiard tables in one big room! Of all these marvels, the gas lights were the most admired, for we were accustomed to the uncertain rays of the two kerosene lamps above our table at Cornwall.

Daly's was the sporting center of Brooklyn, and

in the audience gathered to watch us were a number
of old-time characters of the town.   Tom Gallagher
was there, I think, and Dr. Henry D. Jennings, the
Brooklyn amateur billiard player, who has since become my friend and adviser.

Mr. Daly made us quickly feel at home, and
when the spectators were all in their seats, he introduced us with a gay little speech.

"Frank and Willie Hoppe," he announced, with
a wave of his hand; "the boy wonders of Cornwall.
If they're half as good as their father says they are,
you folks will get your money's worth."

With that, we took our places at the table and
lagged for the break.   When once we had settled
down to the serious business at hand we forgot the
ring of distinguished spectators, the gas lights, the
mahogany bar and all the luxurious trappings of the
place; our world narrowed to a little expanse of
green cloth.   For all that went on outside that small
rectangle, we might have been playing on our old
table at Cornwall, so intent we were upon our game.

Frank got the first ripple of applause when, in the
midst of a run, he tried a bank shot in a side pocket
and made it cleanly.   But the big hand of the evening came toward the end of the game when I was
hopelessly behind and struggling to recover lost
ground.   I was confronted with a difficult cut shot
in a corner pocket.   There was no way to reach it

from the floor, so I scrambled upon the table and lay at full length. And now there was a double problem ahead; to hit the object ball at a fine angle, and then get out of the way of the cue ball on its rapid journey back from the lower rail.

I took aim and fired away. Then, without waiting to see the result, I rolled over and flopped on all fours down on the floor. A roar of laughter greeted me as I arose, not so much for the shot itself as the tumbling feat that accompanied it.

After that Frank and I often practised that acrobatic feat of bouncing off the table on all fours to escape the cue ball. In an exhibition it never failed to get a laugh.

A reporter for the *Brooklyn Eagle* was present at Daly's that night, and the following piece appeared in the paper next morning:

## "YOUNGSTERS PLAY GOOD BILLIARDS

### "FRANK AND WILLIE HOPPE BEGIN THEIR EXHIBITION AT DALY'S

"Many local billiard enthusiasts availed themselves of the opportunity to watch the two young phenomena, Frank and Willie Hoppe play their favorite game at Daly's Academy last night. The diminutive size of the two boys caused some misgivings, but the way they rattled off combination shots, made the double kiss-off and other difficult shots soon put the spectators on the keen edge of excitement. The game was 100 points up and was completed in 13 frames. Willie, the younger of the two, was a little off in his play, but braced up toward the close, being defeated by only 23 points. The actions of the two when they missed reminded the old timers of well known veterans. The score:

Frank Hoppe

  11 12 9 10 8 9 7 10 1 7 5 8 3—100

Willie Hoppe

  4 3 6 3 6 5 8 4 14 8 10 7 0— 77

The two lads will play again tonight."

Maurice Daly had taken a keen interest in the game, and when it was over he patted me on the head and said:

"Willie, that stroke of yours is better adapted to caroms than the pocket game. You have the making of a fine billiard player if you'll study the game and practise."

He told my father that he had watched me closely through the match and had seen me several times stop and ponder, figuring the best shot for position, instead of shooting impulsively like my brother Frank, who was the better shot maker of the two.

"I'd make a carom billiard player of him," Mr.

Daly told my father, just before we started on the return journey to Cornwall, and my father nodded. So it was Maurice Daly who first recognized my billiard talent and started me on the right track.   I can never thank him enough.

From that night on, my career took a new course.

# CHAPTER IV

## SETTLING DOWN TO THE CAROM GAME

My father brought four ivory billiard balls back to Cornwall, when we returned from our first exhibition matches at Daly's. Our old table in the barber shop was the combination variety, which could be changed into a carom table by inserting blocks in the pockets. Following Mr. Daly's advice, I dropped the pocket game and tried my hand at caroms.

There is all the difference in the world between the two games. In stroke, strategy and general execution they are totally unlike. But the chief difference lies in the point of concentration. In the pocket game, the player concentrates upon the object ball and he is concerned chiefly with the course it takes after the cue ball strikes it. In caroms, it is the cue ball and its course with which the player is chiefly concerned.

The pocket stroke is delivered sharply, crisply, to convey the player's intention without any quibbling

to the object ball.   The billiard stroke may be anything from a whip-lash to a caress.

At the age of eight years and two months I was
too young and carefree to be concerned with any of
these nice distinctions, however.   And when my
father placed the three ivory balls upon the table
and told me to make my cue ball connect with the
other two, I tackled it with confidence and enthusiasm.

As Mr. Daly had predicted, my wrist stroke was
much better adapted to billiards than to the free-
swinging game of pocket billiards.   Within a few
weeks I was making double figure runs with regularity.

My father's ambition to make a great billiard
player of me met with mild opposition from my
mother, but as I continued to improve, and as our
exhibitions were bringing in an occasional $5 or $10
to swell the family coffers, she gradually yielded.

No maestro ever drilled a young music pupil
more severely than my father drilled me.   Hour
after hour, until my right arm was so weary it
could scarcely hold the cue he kept me at my task.
Practice, practice, practice; the rail nurse, the anchor,
and the massé, until I fell asleep at night still weav-
ing those ivory balls down the rail in and out, drive
and block and kiss.

Now, as I look back at those long afternoons of

practice in the Cornwall barber shop, I realize that all
the time I was acquiring a billiard instinct, a sub-
conscious control of the balls that was to serve me
faithfully in later years.

Frank wasn't very keen for billiards. He would
much rather play the pocket game. So my father
decided to let each of us develop his own specialty.

One of the first carom exhibitions that I gave was
at the Union League Club in New York City.
Maurice Daly made the arrangements, and when I
arrived in the city that night I found that he had
bought a little tuxedo jacket for me to wear.

"These Union League folks are tony," he told
me, "and you've got to dress up a bit for them."

A clean white shirt, black bow tie and a shoe shine
completed the process of dressing up, and when Mr.
Daly took me in a hansom cab to Fifth Avenue,
Cornwall wouldn't have recognized her barber's son.

This was vastly different from the billiard room
in Brooklyn, or any other billiard room I had played
in. There were oil paintings on the wall and thick
rugs on the floor. The furnishings were rich and
luxurious. And every member had on his dinner
clothes. But if they were "tony," they were cordial
as well.

Mr. Daly held me on his lap while my opponent
was shooting and every time I missed, he would
whisper a word of friendly advice in my ear. After

the exhibition a dozen of the club members took me upstairs in the kitchen and made me an omelette, and before I left, they made up a purse of $50 for me. That was more money than I had ever seen before, and I carried it back to Cornwall Landing as proudly as if it had been a fortune.

In the Spring of 1896, my father arranged an exhibition at the Palatine Hotel, Newburgh. We played billiards on a 4½ by 9 table, without any restrictions save the crotch nurse. I made a run of 310 at straight rail, and a run of 36 at cushion caroms, averaging 3 at the latter game.

It was that exhibition that made my father finally decide to give up the hotel and barber shop, and devote his time wholly to exploiting our talents on the road.

I had not yet seen any of the great masters play billiards, so the foundation of my game was due largely to my father's advice and my own instinct. He had a methodical German mind and he had played enough billiards to understand the principles of the rail nurse, which was the great scoring system in the nineties, and the general theory of position play.

These he drilled into my head by long hours of patient tutoring. He would place the balls for a one-cushion gather shot, and tell me how it would be made. No matter whether I made it the first time or

A Free Hand Massé

not, he would replace the balls and have me try again, until I could not only gather the balls accurately, but land perfectly on the second object ball.

Frank often rebelled at these tedious lessons. During the summer months he would slip away and go swimming down the river, or play baseball up in the village, while I kept at my stint around the billiard table, under the watchful eye of my father.

When fall came, we were ready to fare forth again, this time in earnest. Again my mother made a feeble protest, and again she yielded. We made arrangements with the school authorities to take our books with us, and keep in close touch with our studies.

My father sold his barber shop and the lunch room. We stored what little furniture we had in Grandfather Hoffman's barn, and early in October we quit Cornwall Landing for the wide world, trading the substantial income of the small hotel for the uncertain earning power of a couple of billiard cues wielded by two boys, the eldest of whom was only 11, and the youngest, barely 9.

# CHAPTER V

## THE HOPPE FAMILY GOES ON TOUR

THE only condition on which my mother would consent to breaking up our home in Cornwall was that she be permitted to go along on our travels, and take care of Frank and me. This was the arrangement we worked out:

My father travelled on ahead, booking the dates and arranging for our hotel accommodations, while my mother brought up the rear with us boys, collecting the tickets at exhibitions, checking up the receipts and hearing our lessons. She also was charged with seeing that we practised an hour or two each day, an arrangement which Frank and I found greatly to our liking after the stern discipline of my father.

So we started out, bravely, to seek the family fortunes on the green cloth.

One of the first towns we made was Princeton, N. J. The roomkeeper (I believe his name was Bang) had a big crowd of college students and half a dozen members of the Princeton faculty to watch us play. When the exhibition was over, one of the professors put his fingers on my skull and announced that I had a brachycephalous head, which meant that it was broader than it was long. Jacob Schaefer, the old Wizard, and George Sutton, too, were brachycephals, he said, and he believed that broad-headed people played better billiards than others.

Another professor who asked me a number of questions about the game, said that I had a sub-conscious mathematical mind that could calculate angles instinctively, without resort to the slower and more laborious processes of measuring with the eye from various positions.

I can't remember what I replied to all these profound conclusions, but my mother was deeply impressed, and she wrote all about it to my father the next day. Truly we were getting up in the world, to attract the attention of learned Princeton professors. I wondered what the boys back at Cornwall Landing would have said if they heard I was a brachycephal.

On to Easton, Pennsylvania, thence south through Philadelphia and Westward into a country that had not heard anything about us, and was extremely skeptical about our ability. Sometimes it was difficult to secure bookings. Sometimes we played in the smallest, meanest billiard room in a small, mean town.

Occasionally we had to lay over for a day or two while my father travelled from one city to another in an attempt to secure an engagement. We couldn't afford to stop at the best hotels. Not infrequently when funds were low my father would arrange for us to stop with some private family, where we would get our meals and lodging at a reasonable rate.

My mother was a patient, untiring companion through all our ups and downs. Although we were deprived of a home, she made it her business to see that we got the benefit of a wholesome, domestic routine. We were up early in the mornings, hurrying to the railroad stations with our little satchels, and cues, if we had to move on that day to the next town. If not, my mother would take us for a long walk, returning to the billiard room in time for an hour's practice before lunch.

In the afternoon we studied our lessons, and had another practice session at the table. Frequently we had afternoon exhibitions to play, and then the lessons were cut short.

The receipts for our exhibitions varied as greatly as the character of the billiard rooms we played in. Sometimes we would get a flat guarantee of $15 or $25 from the roomkeeper. Sometimes he would give us $10 and all that was taken in at the door.

Once in a great while the receipts would run up as high as $50 for a single day's exhibitions, and then what a gala feast the Hoppe family would have that night!

Out of the money she collected from the room-keepers, my mother would keep enough for our own living expenses and railroad fare, and send the remainder, if there was any remainder, on ahead to my father.   Frank and I were too young to be bothered about financial affairs, but I still have a vivid recollection of the periods of depression that would fall upon the family when receipts slumped away down and we had scarcely enough for breakfast and railroad fare.

Meanwhile, the newspapers through Pennsylvania, West Virginia, Ohio and Indiana were printing notices of our exhibitions, and gradually the fame of the Hoppe Brothers, Boy Billiardists, was spreading further afield.   By the time we were ready to invade Chicago my father had saved enough from our earnings to purchase two small tuxedo jackets, with black waistcoats and trousers to match.   And we had our pictures taken, decked out in this professional attire.

# CHAPTER VI

### I LEARN A VALUABLE LESSON FROM FRANK IVES, THE YOUNG NAPOLEON

It was in Chicago, during the winter of 1897-98, while we were playing a series of exhibitions at Pop Anson's billiard room that I first saw Frank Ives. Of course, I had heard a great deal about him from my father, who had often seen him play, and in Maurice Daly's room in New York they had told many stories about the "Young Napoleon" that made a deep impression on me.

Ives was a champion roller skater, a champion bicycle rider, a horseman of note, and a great baseball catcher before he took up billiards. Old time sportsmen maintain that he was the greatest all around professional athlete that ever lived. When he reached the top in billiards, around 1891, he gave up the other sports and devoted himself to mastering the ivories.

Maurice Daly says that Ives had the most remarkable pair of eyes ever possessed by any human being.  At the race track, watching the horses line up at the pole a half a mile away, Ives could pick out his horse and rider instantly, while others around him peered in vain through high-powered glasses.

Transferred to the billiard table, this remarkable vision enabled him to land with precision on the thin edge of a ball where other players were content with any kind of a carom.  In addition to keen eyesight, he had the most remarkable power of concentration.  Billiards was an intellectual study to him : he would spend hours mastering some abstract problem of close position play.

When he had won the championship from Jacob Schaefer and beaten all the other foremost players in this country, Ives looked around for new worlds to conquer.  He made a trip to England and spent several weeks studying the English game.  John Roberts was the English champion then, and in April, 1893 Ives challenged him to a match at 6,000 points.  Articles were signed and they were to meet during Derby Week, the following June.

Returning to this country, Ives obtained an English billiard table, 6 x 12, with six pockets, and spent several weeks in secret practice.  When he sailed for England, he told his friends in New York to bet any amount on him, that he had solved the English game, and would beat Roberts without difficulty.

Everybody thought he was depending on the rail

nurse, which he had perfected to a remarkable degree, to turn the trick and the wise ones pointed out that the rail nurse was much more difficult on the English table, where six pockets break the continuity of the rails, than on the American table. And Roberts had had so much more experience with the English game that few sporting men gave Ives more than a passing chance.

But Ives had one backer who accompanied him to London and offered the book-makers all the money they would take, until London sportsmen began to suspect the Young Napoleon had something up his sleeve. Here is what happened: for the first three nights Roberts won handily, rolling up 1,000 points each night against Ives's 689, 981, 573. Then on the fourth night, in the opening inning Ives ran the balls along the rail to the corner pocket and by careful nursing and close manipulation squeezed them into the jaw, where they lodged fast. Then he played his cue-ball back and forth, back and forth while the referee grew hoarse from counting. He ran 2,540 points in that position, and only broke them up when the finish of the game was in sight.

It was Ives's nature, then, to turn around and teach the rail nurse and the "crotch" to Roberts, and give him a return engagement in this country. They played two more matches and broke even.

But I started out to tell about my own experience

with the Young Napoleon in Chicago. He watched
me play an exhibition match with my brother Frank,
and after the game shook me warmly by the hand.

"Now," he said, "come over here in the corner, I
want to show you something." He took a set of
balls and placed them on the table. He showed me
where I had let them get out into the middle panel
during one of my runs. "Never let them pass the
spot," he said. "What's the use of playing on a
table 5 by 10 when you can make a table 2½ by 5
by keeping them below the spot?" Then he showed
me several ways to "go through" the balls in the
open table, so that I could turn them around and
march them down toward the end rail again. I
don't believe there is any player living today who
could play that end table system more consistently
than Ives.

I thanked him, and practised religiously on that
point for many weeks, with gratifying results.

Less than two years later I was to learn of the
Young Napoleon's premature death at Progresso,
Mexico, a victim of tuberculosis. My father told me
afterward that it was drink and dissipation that
killed him.

"Frank Ives thought he was a superman," my
father said; "he thought he could drink twice as
much whiskey as anybody else, and still retain his
steady nerve and his health. That's why he's dead

at thirty-three.   You remember the end-table game he showed you at Cap Anson's in Chicago?   That was a valuable lesson.   Let his untimely death be a lesson to you, too, Willie, and never touch a drop of liquor."

So I am doubly indebted to poor Frank Ives, one of the greatest billiard players that ever lived.

# CHAPTER VII

## TRAVEL AND ADVENTURE

THERE was plenty of variety in our life on the road. No two billiard tables were quite the same, and we were called upon to play with balls of assorted shapes and sizes. In a little Ohio town the room keeper handed us a set of ivory that had seen long service. The two white balls varied nearly a quarter of an inch in diameter.

I had the smaller of the two for my cue ball. After the first few strokes I discovered that I could make the most amazing draw shots with very little effort. But follow shots were almost out of the question. That little ball simply would not follow one of the object balls without a prodigious amount of "top." So I had to readjust my game accordingly and by playing all draw shots and cushion caroms, made a very creditable average.

There were differences, too, in cushions and cloth. Occasionally we would strike a brand new cloth and fast cushions, a combination that we greatly enjoyed although it made scoring difficult. Again we would find a cloth old and worn with the nap gone and the surface consequently slow and uncertain. On an old cloth, where the balls "settle," you can nurse them for long runs with a fairly delicate stroke.

From one town to another it was necessary to adjust our game to changing conditions. And although Frank and I used to growl and grumble like a couple of prima donnas, we were getting valuable experience. The ability to readjust my stroke to meet the eccentricities of ivory and cloth has been a big factor in my championship career.

A room keeper in Springfield, Mass., engaged us to give an exhibition at the opening of his new establishment. He paid us a flat guarantee of $25 and invited the public to come without admission charge to see his fine place.

When the hour arrived for our exhibition the crowd was so great the police had to be summoned to make a lane from the door for Frank and me to reach the table. They were standing on tables, hanging to cue racks, perched in every nook and cranny around the wall. They even climbed all over the poor man's electric piano, kicking out the stained glass panels with their heels.

When the exhibition was over and the crowd had gone, the room keeper surveyed a sorry sight. The cue-racks had been pulled loose from the walls, the tables had been trampled and burned with cigarette stubs; everywhere was ruin and desolation.

But the room keeper was a philosopher. When we told him that was the biggest crowd we had ever played for, in all our travels, he was greatly elated. He lit a cigar and said:

"Well, if one-tenth of 'em come back and try some of the tricks you boys showed 'em, I'll get my money back."

In Carthage, Mo., we had among the spectators, a very distinguished looking individual with a black beard and frock coat. When our exhibition was over he came up to my mother and said:

"I'm a hypnotist. I can hypnotize that boy of yours so he'll fall asleep."

"Hump!" said my mother.

"I can hypnotize him," the black-bearded man went on, "so's he'll never be able to play billiards again."

"Nonsense!" said my mother.

"Or," said the hypnotist, "I can hypnotize him so he'll be the greatest billiard player that ever lived."

My father, who was standing near, broke into the conversation. "You say you can hypnotize Willie so he'll play a better game of billiards?" he asked.

"Certainly," said the black-bearded man. "I can

hypnotize him so he can play billiards with his eyes shut.   Him or anybody else."

"Look here, stranger," he said finally; "I'll make *you* a proposition.   You take any other boy and cast your spell onto him.   Hypnotize him as much as you want and make him as good a billiard player as you can.   Then," said my father, putting his hand on my shoulder, "I'll back Willie against him for a thousand dollars!"

The hypnotist didn't take up the offer, which was just as well because my father didn't have a thousand dollars to put up, but he retreated in some confusion.   My mother worried about the incident, in spite of her skepticism, and she warned me not to be attracted to the gaze of frock-coated strangers with black beards, and piercing eyes.

So, in big town and little towns, my billiard education progressed and my contacts with life reached out in an ever-widening circle.   Each day I had a strange billiard table to solve, and each day some new problem in the mastery of three ivory balls arose to keep my young mind busy.

# CHAPTER VIII

## MY MOTHER TAKES A HAND AT THE GAME

FRANK grew tired of life on the road. Perhaps it was my father's stern discipline; more likely, he did not possess the keen enthusiasm for billiards that kept my interest in the game alive. At any rate, when we returned to Cornwall in the spring of 1900, after a long trip around the country, Frank announced that he was going to study stenography and go into business.

That left me without a playing partner. We held a family conference at Grandfather Hoffman's house and it was decided that my mother should learn the game and take Frank's place in our little billiard troupe.

A year or two before, the Brunswick-Balke-Collender Company had made me a present of a fine 5 by 10 billiard table. Cornwall was still our family headquarters, so we set the table up in a large loft in my Grandfather's barn and there I used to practise during the summer months.

My mother now shared those long practise hours

with me.  My father and I took turns teaching her how to hold the cue, how to draw and follow and control the dead ball.  She showed surprising aptitude for the game.  Before many weeks she was making runs of fifteen and twenty with regularity. In addition, she mastered a number of fancy shots for exhibition purposes.

In October we fared forth again.  New York was our first stop and Maurice Daly was again our host for a series of exhibition matches.  This time we played at his big room at Thirty-first Street and Broadway, now occupied by Joe Thum's Academy.

The novelty of a woman billiard player drew quite a crowd to Daly's and when we were introduced and made ready to string for the break, two or three hundred onlookers had gathered to watch us.  I was playing 100 or no count to my mother's straight billiards.  In other words, I had to reach 100 in a single run before she could accumulate the same number in separate innings.

My mother won the bank and missed the opening shot.  I had an easy one cushion shot for position and gathered them nicely on the rail.  Of course I had to play my best no matter who was holding the other cue.  I reached the first hundred in a little more than five minutes of play, and was well started on the second when an accidental foul stopped me at 119.

WILLIE HOPPE AT THE AGE OF 11 PRACTISING UNDER THE WATCHFUL
EYE OF MAURICE DALY

Mr. Daly, former world's champion, taught the youngster many fine points
of the game.

Poor Mother! She seemed nervous when she stepped to the table again. All the nice strokes and strategy we had taught her in Cornwall had fled from her mind. She made a single carom and sat down. I ran a dozen or so, and then tripped up. Mother succeeded in collecting 8 billiards, one at a time, before I got the balls bunched on the rail again, and ran my second hundred.

In the fancy shot exhibition that followed she regained her nerve, however, and made a number of very difficult massés, winning a hearty burst of applause from the spectators.

During the week that we remained in New York City, Mr. Daly took me in hand for several hours instruction each day. He taught me a lot about second ball play and close position work. He was enthusiastic about the progress I had made and he said to my father:

"Frank, I can't teach that boy of yours anything about billiards. He knows as much as I do right now. The only thing I might show him is how to use a bridge, but he won't touch one."

My father explained that I had been spoiled, as far as the use of the bridge was concerned. Having permitted me to climb all over the table as a small boy, he couldn't break me of the habit now that I had grown to the mature age of 13. And it was a fact that I would never touch a bridge when the leniency of the referee would let me climb up and lie flat on the table.

My mother's game improved after we had left New York. She made several creditable runs, the highest being 36.

Meanwhile my own game was undergoing a thorough revision, because I had mastered straight rail and the rail nurse, and was beginning to experiment with the balk line, the recognized professional test for billiard players. At every opportunity, I had the lines drawn on the table and practised under the balk line restrictions.

In the game of 14.2 which was standard at that time, the lines are drawn 14 inches from each cushion and the player is allowed two shots in the restricted space. On the second shot he must drive one of the object balls across the line, or he forfeits his point and turn.

Whereas, in straight rail, the great problem was to get the balls together on the rail, now my objective was to gather them near the balk lines, preferably astride the line where they could be nursed without penalty. This new problem added zest to the game, and kept me continually on edge, both during practise and exhibition matches to experiment.

# CHAPTER IX

## I TURN PROFESSIONAL AND MEET MY FIRST REAL TEST

At length, in the year 1901, there came a time when my billiard skill had to meet a real test. Up to that time I had been a prodigy in short pants, a smart youngster whom people came to watch more because of his diminutive size and clever antics than for serious professional skill.

It was easy enough in my matches against Frank and my mother to make runs of fifty and a hundred. It was easy enough to make fancy massé shots and four cushion gathers before a small-town audience that sat, wide-eyed and open-mouthed, waiting to be astonished and eager to applaud. It was easy to climb all over the table and make shots from all angles when there was nothing at stake.

But now came the real test; could I play sound, consistent billiards against the recognized professionals? Could I hold my own against an opponent who depended on billiards for a livelihood, who was as eager to win as I and to whom each button on the wire meant dollars and cents?

In October, 1901, a few days after my fourteenth birthday, my father and I journeyed down from Cornwall Landing to New York City. Maurice Daly was arranging a "short-stop" professional tournament as a preliminary to the winter billiard season, and after a conference over handicaps, it was decided I should enter.

"He needs tournament experience," Mr. Daly told my father; "let's see what he can do in fast company."

The other players entered were Thomas Gallagher, Ed McLaughlin, Ora Morningstar and Jose Ortiz. The first two were widely known American professionals of the second rank, veterans of many a tournament and match. Morningstar was a young player in his twenties, who under the tutelage of Frank Ives had shown great promise. Those three were to play for 300 points. Ortiz was a newcomer from Spain. On the basis of his showing in practise matches Mr. Daly rated him at 225, while I had to play for 200.

Two weeks of constant practice under the watchful eyes of my father and Mr. Daly put me on keen edge for the fray. We were to play 18.1, a game that permits only one shot in the restricted spaces and practically bars close manipulation near the rails.

But I had learned the trick of gathering them near the lines, and was confident of holding my own with any of them on 1-cushion shots and open table play.

Ortiz and I met in the first match of the tournament the night of October 21. After the formalities—Mr. Daly always started his affairs with a flourish—we stood at the table to bank for the break.

To my astonishment, my ball rolled back from the lower rail at a snail's pace and stopped just above the spot. I had lost the bank by about eighteen inches, and Ortiz had the first shot. As I went to my seat, I wondered why I had failed so miserably to gauge the speed of the table, and I looked toward my father expecting to receive a stern reproof. But he had lighted a cigar and settled himself comfortably in his seat. My mother gave me a reassuring smile.

Ortiz missed the opening shot and left me fairly easy. I gathered six on my first turn at the table and left them scattered. After several innings of "jockeying," during which neither of us could get the balls under control, I launched on my first run with a 15 in the seventh, and came back with 26 in the eighth. Ortiz seemed nervous and his uncertainty gave me confidence. Toward the end of the game I was shooting with my old time assurance and a 44 in the thirtieth inning put the game safely "on ice."

Here is the score of my first tournament match:

Hoppe:

> 6   1 0 0 0 15 26 2 3 2 1   1 0 9   7
> 0 18 2 0 9   3   1 4 1 0 2 25 0 1 10
> 44   0 7—Total, 200; high runs, 44, 26,
> 25; average 6 2-33

Ortiz:

> 0 0 0 6 6 0 0 1 2 0 13   6 12 1 0
> 8 2 1 0 5 0 3 1 0 7   5 10   0 2 3
> 3 3 0—Total, 101; high run, 13;
> average 3 2-33

The referee of that first match was Mark Muldauer, the amateur who has competed in a number of Class A tournaments and still ranks high in the Metropolitan district.

My next opponent was Tom Gallagher, the veteran. He tried safety tactics, and whenever he missed the balls were widely separated. But I was fortunate enough to get in several good runs, and my average against him was even better than in the first game. Gallagher made only 125 of his 300 points while I was scoring 200. I had a high run of 54, while his best was 42, and I averaged 7 18-26 to his 4.

To make a long story short, I went through the tournament without losing a game, beating all my opponents better than even except McLaughlin, who made 295 of his 300 before I scored my 200th point. Toward the close of the game McLaughlin got the balls rolling nicely and scored 148 points in three innings, with one high run of 89.

But my early lead was too much for him, and I ran out when he needed only 5.

The $300 which I won as first prize came in very handily, but as I look back now upon that first test of my game, the most valuable thing I gained was confidence. I had been able to hold a steady cue against some of the best billiardists in the game; and that meant a great deal to me.

When the tournament was finished, Mr. Daly said:

"Well, Willie, you've done pretty well. Now I'm going to match you against a famous Frenchman who has come over for the World's Championship."

And a few days later the papers carried the announcement of a special match between Willie Hoppe, the "Boy Wonder," and Louis Barutel.

# CHAPTER X

## MATCHES WITH BARUTEL; A TRIP TO NEW ORLEANS

It is the winter of 1901-1902. I have arrived at the age of 14. Back in Cornwall my schoolmates are studying Latin and Algebra, helping with the chores at home, playing hockey and hookey, building snow forts in the school yard, adventuring out on the river ice, hunting rabbits on the old Read farm. But those boyish pastimes are not for me..

I am in another world. Here I sit in Daly's Billiard Academy. The roar of Broadway comes faintly through the window, but I do not hear it. My ears are tuned to the click of ivory balls. My father sits near me, and around the billiard table is a fringe of spectators, with Maurice Daly hovering in the background.

Through a blue mist of cigar smoke I am watching a distinguished gentleman with a pointed black beard and curled mustaches. He is flourishing a billiard cue. He shoots; I watch the ball spin back in a graceful curve and glide off the cushion to the second object ball.

The balls are close together.   Monsieur Barutel
—for the gentleman with the black beard is none
other—lifts his cue for a massé.   He makes a tripod
with the fingers of his left hand.   The cue rises and
falls half a dozen times in a quick preliminary
flourish as he takes his aim.   Then with a crunch
the cue tip bites sharply into the ivory.   The ball
darts away and suddenly circles back, completing
the carom on the two object balls with niceness and
precision.

Presently Monsieur Barutel misses.   He sits
down, murmuring some phrases in French.   I do
not understand the words, but from the shrug of his
shoulders and his general demeanor I gather that
the balls are possessed of devils, and that there is a
conspiracy in the high heavens against one M.
Barutel.

I go to the table and chalk my cue.   With a
cushion carom and a draw shot or two I gather the
balls near the lower rail.   My father looks on ap-
provingly; Maurice Daly wags his head in a gesture
of encouragement; and so I continue, with youthful
assurance.

Such are my random impressions of the two
matches with Louis Barutel played in the winter of
my fourteenth year.   That winter was important
in my billiard education in other respects, for in
December all the great billiard players of the coun-

try gathered at Madison Square Garden for a
world's championship at 18.1 and I was permitted
to watch all the games from a ring-side seat.

Six experts were entered in the tournament;
Jacob Schafer, the "Wizard," Ora Morningstar,
Leonard Howison of Canada, George F. Slosson,
Barutel and George Sutton. Schaefer finished first,
winning five straight matches with a grand average
of 7.78 and a high run of 68. Sutton's grand average was 9.26, but he finished only fourth.

That inconsistency illustrates one of the vagaries
of billiards; a good match player may win all his
games as Schaefer did, and yet fall below the others
in grand average figures.

Sitting at the edge of the table through every
game of the tournament I was able to study the
styles of the different players and watch the various
methods they employed. I don't suppose I stopped
to analyze these methods or results, but I learned a
great deal by just sitting there and absorbing, like a
young sponge, all the billiards in the vicinity.

Whenever the Wizard raised his cue for a massé
my arm went up in imagination, too, and I played
the shot mentally along with him. Whenever Sutton gathered the balls in a close nursing position in
the center panel, and edged his cue ball softly back
and forth, my right wrist twitched, for I was nursing them, too.

When the tournament was finished, my father made preparations to take me on the road again. This time we headed south.  Parson Davies of New Orleans, a well known sporting character who ran a billiard room, had seen me play at Daly's earlier in the winter and he made my father an offer of $100 a week and railroad fare if he would journey down to New Orleans.

We reached New Orleans in January, 1902.  The racing season was at its height and the old southern city was filled with gamblers, book-makers, and camp followers of the ponies.  Davies's establishment was the sporting headquarters, and every evening the race-track crowd would come back from Jefferson Park to try their luck at the card tables, and incidentally, to watch me play billiards.

Mr. Davies had a great idea.  When we arrived in New Orleans I found he had built a little wooden platform around the billiard table, for me to stand on.  I found this a great help in reaching awkward shots in the middle of the table, but it was hard on my opponents.  They had to take their stance with one foot on the floor and one on the platform, and their balance consequently was anything but secure.

I played exhibition matches for two weeks in New Orleans, and when we were ready to start on tour again, my father engaged an advance agent to go ahead and secure bookings and take care of the publicity. He was an old fellow by the name of Luckie. His first stop was Memphis. When we arrived there my father met him at the hotel to discuss the arrangements he had made. They talked about the price of tickets, the advance sale, and other details, and my father asked him if the exhibition had been well advertised.

"Certainly," said Mr. Luckie; "of course."

"You've been to all the newspaper offices?"

'Well, no," said Mr. Luckie, "I didn't think it was necessary."

"What!" said my father in astonishment, "then how in the world have you advertised the exhibition?"

Mr. Luckie explained that he had spent a great deal of time around the billiard room and the hotel lobby, telling everybody he met about the "Boy Wonder" who was to play billiards in Memphis.

"And they've all promised to come," he assured us.

Well, that was the end of Mr. Luckie. We shipped him back to New Orleans, and fared on northward, to St. Louis.

# CHAPTER XI

## OUR FORTUNES AT LOW EBB—THE TIDE TURNS

WE had rough sledding on the road that year. Mr. Luckie's failure to make good as an advance agent made my father's job doubly difficult. All I had to do was to adjust my game to the differences of cloth and cushion on each new table, and to make the three ivory balls behave; but my father had to make all the booking arrangements, sell tickets, distribute hand bills, tack up posters, visit the newspaper offices and at the same time keep a watchful eye on me, for I was still too young to travel alone.

I can remember him sitting in the lobby of some little hotel in a Middle Western town, chewing the frayed end of a cigar, studying a map and a railroad time table, wondering which town to make on our next jump, figuring up the railroad fare and counting a little bundle of bills—mostly ones and twos—to see whether we had money enough to make it.

In spite of the fact that I had gained something

of a reputation by this time—and my father always carried around a bunch of newspaper clippings to prove it—the room keepers were skeptical of my ability and slow to guarantee purses for our exhibitions.

We arrived in a Missouri town on the same day that Barnum and Bailey's circus played an engagement there. We went to the afternoon performance, and while we were in the side-show tent, watching the freaks, my father had an idea.

He hunted up the manager of the circus and introduced himself.

"I'm Frank Hoppe," he said, "and this is Willie Hoppe, the Boy Wonder, the greatest young billiard player in the world. Here's a great idea. Put a billiard table in your side show tent, and let my boy give an exhibition at every performance."

The circus manager had a faraway look in his eye.

"Look here," my father went on, warming up to his subject, "this sword swallowing is old stuff. So is the bearded lady. The people are tired of snake charmers and fire eaters. Why don't you give them something new? My boy can take three ivory balls and make a hundred points with the rail nurse in five minutes. Look at these clippings," and he produced his bundle of newspaper publicity.

The circus manager explained that the country people could see billiards played every time they came to town. Billiard balls and cues were familiar objects. What the circus wanted to do was to get away from everyday things and give the people something strange and romantic. "Now if your Willie could wear a Hindu juggler's costume, balance a couple of balls on the end of his nose and then make fancy shots at the same time, we might be able to make a place for him."

My father's enthusiasm waned. The circus, with all its grandeur and glitter and noise, went on its way without us, and my father returned to the prosaic job of selling my billiard skill to a skeptical public, in billiard rooms where they spoke our language and wore plain clothes.

We ran into a stretch of hard luck soon after that. Receipts fell off, and we had to write home for money. Finally, when we reached Moberly, Mo., we were down to our last dollar. My father canvassed the billiard rooms of the town without any success. Nobody apparently wanted to see me play. The proprietor of the biggest room in town was particularly obstinate. My father argued with him for nearly an hour, trying to make a deal.

"This ain't a vaudeville show," said the room keeper. "Why should I spend my good money to get a crowd here just to see your boy play? Besides, how do I know he can do all the things you say?"

My father offered to cut the fee from $25 to $15,

then $10, and finally, in desperation, he offered to give the exhibition for what he could collect from the crowd. The room keeper was obstinate. He wouldn't budge.

"Well," my father finally said, "will you let us have the use of a table for him to practice on?" The proprietor grudgingly agreed. So that night, after we had spent our last dollar for supper, we went back to the billiard room, and my father handed me the ivory balls we carried with us.

"Willie, my boy," he said in German, "show these people what you can do."

I started in. A little crowd collected. The room keeper paid no attention at first, but after a while he left his desk and came over to watch. My father sat sullenly in a corner, grumbling to himself.

As for me, I don't believe I ever played better billiards in my life. The balls were in a particularly amiable mood, and I marched them down the rail, turned the corner and marched them back again, making points almost as fast as I could stroke my cue.

At the end of an hour my father tapped me on the shoulder.

"Come on, Willie," he said, "it's time to go." The crowd, which had grown to more than a hundred, wanted me to keep on playing. But my father shook his head.

"Hold on," said the room keeper. He went to his cash register and took out a $5 bill. Others in the crowd offered to chip in. But now it was my father's turn to be obstinate.

"Willie," he said, "put up your cue." Then he turned to the room keeper. "Keep your $5," he said. "I gave you a chance to make a deal, but you turned me down. Now you can't hire him with all the money in this town." And we marched grandly out of the place.

At the hotel that night, we found two letters. One had a foreign postage stamp. Jacob Schaefer, the Wizard, who had gone to Paris after winning the world's championship in New York City in December, wrote to say that he had made a deal with the manager of one of the big Paris academies for me to go abroad and play some of the young French experts. I would receive $300 a month and all my expenses.

The other letter was postmarked "Cornwall." It contained a money order. My mother had pawned her diamond ring to pay our railroad fare back to New York.

# CHAPTER XII

## OFF TO PARIS!

As a result of Jacob Schaefer's negotiations, I sailed for France in October, 1902, to begin a series of engagements at the Olympia Academy in Paris. The trip was too expensive for my father, so he stayed at home. It was arranged that John Kammerer, Schaefer's father-in-law who was returning to Paris at the same time, should look out for me on the journey across, and I was to live with the Kammerers at their home in Paris.

My father and mother, Frank, and my two sisters were at the pier to see me off. My father delivered a lot of last-minute instructions to Kammerer just before we went on board. I must practice two hours every morning and be in bed by 10.30 every night. No gallivanting around the boulevards; no smoking, no drinking. My salary was to be sent back home every week, after deducting just enough to pay my board and incidental expenses.

With these final admonitions ringing in my ears, and my mother trying to comfort my sisters, who were crying as heartily as she, we set sail.

I caught a last glimpse of my family as the *Fuerst Bismarck* swung out in midstream and headed down the bay. They were standing in a group at the end of the Hoboken pier, waving handkerchiefs and shouting farewell messages which I could not hear, but only guess at. And yet I knew what they were calling to me, however faintly the sounds came floating across the water.

My mother was telling me to be a good boy and say my prayers. My father was telling me to remember and practice at least two hours every morning. And Frank's farewell was something like this: "Beat those Frenchmen, Willie, or don't ever come back!"

Mr. Kammerer, undisturbed by any sentimental reflections, settled himself comfortably in the smoking room as the steamer dropped down the Narrows. As soon as the New York sky line had disappeared I went on a tour of exploration. The first thing that occurred to me, of course, was to look for the billiard room. Surely every first class ocean liner would be equipped with a couple of billiard tables, and I looked forward to putting in several hours of practice each day on the journey across.

I must have traversed several miles of passageways, and climbed a dozen flights of stairs looking for that billiard room. But there wasn't any. Finally, when I asked Mr. Kammerer about it, he explained that they hadn't yet been able to find a way to keep the ocean smooth, and as long as the ship rolled and tossed, you couldn't get the billiard balls to stay in one spot long enough to make a shot.

So, for the first time in seven years, I had a vacation from the billiard table.

Mr. Kammerer and I used to take long walks around the deck, and he would tell me about the famous French players, Maurice Vignaux, the old Master, and Louis Cure, Firmin Cassignol, a young player who was said to possess perfect form at the table, Sanchez, and Alvarez. He used to compare these French experts with his son-in-law Jacob Schaefer, who excelled them all, especially in the massé, and of whom he was very proud.

Deck shuffleboard and quoits helped to pass the time on our journey, and also served to keep my eye and hand in trim. The seven days crossing passed quickly enough, and before I could realize it, we had landed at Havre and were on a train, bound for Paris.

I had heard a great deal about the French academies. They were altogether different, I found, from the billiard rooms I had been used to in the United States. The Olympia, where I was under contract to play twice a day for three months, was upstairs over the Olympia Music Hall in the Boulevard des Capucines, just off the Rue Scribe, a quarter well known to all American travellers.

Instead of a large public room, with billiard tables all about, the Olympia Academy consisted chiefly of an amphitheater surrounding a single billiard table, with seats arranged in tiers all about, and little tables scattered about where the spectators could sit and drink their wine.

No admission fee was charged, but every patron, upon entering and taking his seat, was visited by the waiter and he had to invest in at least one drink to the value of a franc. The Frenchmen could make this initial drink go a long ways. One glass of port wine would last the average Parisian billiard enthusiast through two-hundred points of balk-line, twenty points of three cushions and a dozen games of rouge, or red ball.

Upon our arrival in Paris, Mr. Kammerer took me to the manager of the Olympia, and when the introductions were accomplished, he arranged for my first exhibition in public. I was to be given three days for practice, to become accustomed to the new conditions of cloth, balls, lighting, surroundings, etc., and then I was to be matched against the young French player, Fournil.

Meanwhile placards were posted in the cafés, announcing the arrival of "Le Jeune Americaine, Willie Hoppe, Garçon Extraordinaire," who would meet all comers at the Olympia.

# CHAPTER XIII

## REMINISCENCES OF THE PARIS ACADEMIES

THE ivory balls used in France are a fraction of an inch larger than our billiard balls, and the cloth has a heavier nap. Otherwise, the playing conditions are substantially the same. It did not take me long to get my bearings and recover my stroke, after the sea voyage, and when I stepped to the table one October afternoon for my first match against Fournil, I was confident of giving a good account of myself.

French billiard fans had turned out in force to see the "young American in short pants," and there was quite a sprinkling of Americans in the gallery, too. By this time I was thoroughly accustomed to playing before an audience, and the size of the crowd didn't bother me.

More than anything else I missed my father. I had played so long under his watchful eye, that it seemed strange not to find him there at my elbow

every time I sat down, to receive a stern reproof if
I had played badly or a good word if I had done
well.

The match was close, but I managed to make a
good showing.  After playing 200 points of balk
line, we changed the game, as is the French custom,
and played three-cushion caroms and red ball.

The referee counted the points in French, "un,
deux, trois," etc.  Along toward the end of the game
he would say, *"et pour trois,"* meaning "and for
three"; *"et pour deux"*—"and for two," and finally
*"et gagner!"*—"and he wins!"  Thus the game
reached its climax and the referee dramatically gave
warning when the finish was near.

I had my first experience, that afternoon, with
the French system of betting on the games.  When
the players are announced, the patrons sitting around
the amphitheatre are privileged to come forward and
place bets on their favorites.  If one player is considered greatly superior, so that the betting on him
is top heavy, the odds of the game are shortened to
give the poorer player a chance, and this handicap-
ping goes on until the public's judgment is equalized
with the player's skill.

A croupier, presiding at the table, takes all bets;
and the odds are marked on a board on the wall.
This croupier is a remarkable person.  He never
takes a patron's name or makes any elaborate memo-

HOPPE'S $50,000 LEFT HAND FIRMLY PLANTED FOR A SHORT MASSÉ

Three fingers are spread out to form a tripod, and the forefinger is curled up to support the tip of the cue.

randa. Knowing most of the patrons by sight, he keeps track of all the bets in his head, and he pays off with never an error.

If a newcomer should venture a wager, the croupier merely refers to him as Monsieur X. or Monsieur Y., takes his money, and the transaction is complete. His memory of faces is so good that he never pays the wrong man.

It was the custom to stage several minor balk line matches at the Paris academies early in the afternoon, but these were desultory affairs. The real activity commenced between four and five. At that hour your Parisian sportsman is returning to the boulevards from the numerous race courses around the city, all of which are within a half hour's taxi ride. He desires more action, and so he repairs to the billiard academy.

The red ball games, with three players entered, provided a quick and effective method of providing action for the boulevardier. The games were limited to ten or fifteen points and lasted only a few minutes. Betting was lively, and the players received a percentage of the amount wagered on them if they won. The management also took a share.

Red ball is a tricky game. You have to make all your points by striking the red ball first, then completing the carom on the other white ball. Occasionally one of the players would get a lucky streak and run his string out from the break, and the gallery would noisily demonstrate its enthusiasm. Then again, when a player would trip up on what looked like a simple shot, with only one point to go, his backers in the gallery would groan, and protest that they were being tricked, double crossed and swindled.

You couldn't blame a fellow, if he had had a bad day at the race track for being a bit disgruntled when he saw his last handful of francs being swept away by the unlucky roll of a billiard ball, and their hisses were only a natural consequence.

I can remember how Vignaux, the distinguished old Frenchman used to behave on those occasions. He would turn to the gallery, raise his arms and throw back his huge head with its flowing mane of white hair, calling upon whatever gods lurked in the Olympia's dim, smoky ceiling to witness that he had done his best, and hadn't missed the shot on purpose.

Louis Cure, on the other hand, was never perturbed by hisses from the gallery. He would resume his seat and glare at the enraged Frenchmen as much as to say:

"Well, what if I did miss? It is my privilege. What are you going to do about it?" He was utterly impervious to criticism.

As a matter of fact, the games were absolutely

on the level. The players couldn't afford to become involved in any crooked work, because the academy management and the public would be quick to detect and denounce them.

I had a tragedy of my own during one of those red ball sessions. One afternoon two distinguished gentlemen came and sat down near the table. One of them called me over just before the red ball game started.

"Willie," he said, "I'm an American. I've just bet $500 on you to beat that Frenchman. If you win, it's yours."

I went back to my seat in a daze. Leonard Howison, another young American player, was standing nearby, and I said to him,

"There's a party over there who says he's just bet $500 on me, and will give it to me if I win. Is he kidding me?"

Leonard looked across the room where the two strangers sat.

"Hell, no," he said. "That's Charles M. Schwab, the big steel magnate. The other man is his physician. He means it. Go ahead and win."

In the next few minutes, I had figured out all the things I was going to do with that five hundred dollars. First I was going to buy my father the finest meerschaum pipe in Paris. A diamond ring for mother, some dresses for my sisters, and a big yellow walking stick for Frank completed my shopping list.

But when I stepped to the table to shoot, I found I couldn't see the balls, much less hit them right, and I lost the game by a lop-sided score. I never did understand clearly just what happened, or how I came to lose, in an instant, all the billiard instinct I had acquired through seven long years.

I went over to Mr. Schwab and tried to apologize, but he slapped me on the shoulder and didn't seem to mind at all.

I have the satisfaction of knowing that Mr. Schwab was present at another billiard match when I gave a better account of myself. He came to the Pennsylvania Hotel on the last night of the challenge match with Young Jake Schaefer, in March, 1923. Every seat was sold and the standing room space behind the gallery was jammed. But somebody at the door recognized Mr. Schwab, and they found a place for him inside. Then he saw me play one of the finest matches of my career.

# CHAPTER XIV

## TEMPERAMENT AND PANTOMIME

AMONG the American professionals playing in Paris that year was a man named Ben Saylor. When conditions were just right, he could play great billiards, but he was more easily affected by trivial things than any billiard player I have even known. He didn't want the other professionals sitting in the gallery on the days when he was playing. The slightest untoward circumstance would upset his game.

At one end of the Olympia billiard amphitheatre was a back drop, painted to represent a garden scene, and down in one corner was a painted bench. Alvarez, a Spanish professional, had a stiff leg. It was a peculiar property of this leg that enabled Alvarez to sit upon it without requiring a chair or any other support.

During his matches with Saylor, Alvarez, instead

of taking his usual seat in the players' chair would limp over to the painted back drop and pretend to sit down upon the painted bench, supporting himself on the hinge of his crippled leg.

This little by-play would always distract the spectators' attention and throw Saylor off his game.

One afternoon Leonard Howison and I, celebrating an off-day, climbed the little stairway leading to the gallery and seated ourselves in the topmost row of benches, to watch the game without letting Saylor know we were in the house. Alvarez had just finished shooting, and had made his way over to the painted garden and was seated precariously on his imaginary bench.

When Saylor walked to the table, he found his ball frozen to a side cushion. As he took his stance for the shot we could see he was fuming to himself. He drew back his cue to make the preliminary waggle. The butt struck against the little railing that surrounded the table, on which the wine glasses of the ring-side spectators rested.

Saylor had a fiddling stroke, that see-sawed back and forth a good deal before he released it. Now, as he fiddled, every time he drew back the butt of his cue tapped the railing.

Howison nudged me, and I began to giggle. We were both youngsters at the giggling age, and once we started, nothing could stop us. Saylor heard us, and turned around. He glared up at the gallery. He glared at Alvarez, sitting placidly on his leg. Then he turned to the railing.

Crash! With one sweep of his cue he cleaned the board. Red wine, white wine, port wine and beer, bottles, glasses and all went tumbling into the laps of the astonished French spectators. Howison and I got up quietly and tip-toed down the back stairs. We went down to the Olympia Music Hall underneath the Academy, where "The Prince of Pilsen" translated into French was playing, and spent the rest of the afternoon listening to musical comedy. But we didn't see anything half as funny as Ben Saylor's burst of temperament.

Later we learned that the management had Saylor apologize to all of the patrons who had been drenched, and the house bought a drink all around. Alvarez won the game.

Eddie Foy, the American comedian, was a familiar figure around the Paris academies. An enthusiastic billiard player himself, he was on hand for every important match.

They tell a story about a great contest between Frank Ives and Maurice Vignaux, played at the Olympia in 1892, before my time. It was the custom for the French spectators to occupy the tiers of seats on one side of the table, and the foreigners to occupy the opposite side. The French player would sit in a chair in front of his own countrymen, and his opponent would sit across the way.

Ives was not a temperamental player. It took a good deal to disturb his poise. But on this occasion, soon after the match began, he observed a strange commotion in the French gallery. While Vignaux was at the table certain spectators were pointing over in his direction and whispering among themselves. Ives wondered whether they were pointing at him, and if so, what was wrong.

He had several turns at the table, but was unable to get the balls rolling right. Every time he took his seat he would glance up at the French gallery. The agitation among the spectators persisted, and it began to get on his nerves. The whole French side of the audience was engaged in whispering, pointing and laughing. They seemed to be paying very little attention to the game. Was it a conspiracy to rattle Ives and throw him off his stride?

Finally, he chanced to turn around and look over his shoulder. Up midway in the American "bleachers" was Eddie Foy. He was carrying on a little billiard game of his own, imitating the old Frenchman, Vignaux. Every time Vignaux would toss back his lion-like mane of hair Eddie would throw his head back in the same gesture. And as the majestic Frenchman marched around the table, studying the balls from various angles, Eddie, with great seriousness followed his every action in pantomime.

Ives caught the comedian's eye, smiled in recognition, and waved him to be quiet. The commotion in the French gallery ceased abruptly and spectators and players turned again to the game. It seemed that Foy had bet a substantial sum on Ives, and was contributing his own talents to the distraction of the French player. But his little plot very nearly proved a boomerang.

On that first trip the management of the Olympia arranged a Jeune Maître Tournament, for the championship of the Young Masters, and that I won without the loss of a single game. It was intended to make it an annual competition, subject to challenge, but my contract expired soon afterward, and I returned to the United States without being called upon to defend it. So in addition to various other titles it happens that I am the Jeune Maître champion of France.

# CHAPTER XV

DURING my first sojourn in Paris I met nearly all the leading French players at the Olympia. Jacob Schaefer was under contract to play at the Grand Café, the chief rival of the Olympia, and although I lived under the same roof with him, at the home of John Kammerer, we never met in competition.

In December, 1902, the French Government renewed its old hostility toward the billiard academies. Gambling on our exhibition games had increased to such a point that the government felt the popularity of the game was becoming a menace to the young manhood of France.

The matter had been fought out in the courts, and a French judge decided that inasmuch as billiards was primarily a game of skill, it could not be banned as a game of chance. But the government was not content to relinquish its opposition. An order was issued prohibiting foreigners from taking

74

part in exhibition matches at which wagers were laid. The academy managers took this new ruling in court and while the litigation was pending we had some exciting times with the "law."

Being under contract to the Olympia, which had paid my expenses to Paris, I had to abide by the manager's orders. And as I was just turned 15, I did not assume any great activity in the battle of wits with the government.

I was playing a match with Vignaux one afternoon when the doorman appeared suddenly at the edge of the table. He was very much excited.

"Le Commissionaire" he announced in a stage whisper. M. Vignaux seized me by the hand and led me to the rear of the room, where we hid behind the curtain. Presently I peeked out. There stood "Le Commissionaire" of Police, a pompous gentleman in frock coat and a high silk hat, all out of breath from climbing the stairs.

He reached in his breast pocket and brought forth a tri-color scarf, which he waved in the manager's face. "Monsieur le manager," he said, when his breath had returned, "I am the police. Where is this Willie Hoppe?"

The manager looked blankly at him.

"Which Willie Hoppe?"

"Ah," said the official, "You well know who I mean. Your marvelous young American. I have here a Government order which says he shall not play the billiards."

The manager looked all around the table. Then he looked under the table.

"Monsieur le Commissionaire," he said gravely, "I regret that he is not here. I shall communicate to him your desires in the matter. You are fatigued from your journey up the stairs. M. le Com, will you not try a glass of the white wine?" Whereupon the official stalked out. We emerged from behind the curtain, and with a nod from the manager, resumed our game.

On two occasions after that we were honored with visits from the Prefect, but he was so slow in climbing the stairs that we were always safely hid behind the curtain when he arrived.

My contract with the Olympia having at length expired, I took leave of my good friends Mr. and Mrs. Kammerer, bought some souvenirs for my mother and sisters, and packed up my satchel.

As the boat train left the station on my return journey to America, I took stock of my three months' stay in Paris. I had earned nearly a thousand dollars for my family. I had met and conquered the best of the young French professionals.

More important than either of these, I had gained invaluable experience in my daily associations at the Olympia, watching Vignaux measure angles and deliver his strokes with the precision and decisiveness of a great master; analyzing French methods of play and developing an all around game in balk line, three cushions and red ball.

Besides this billiard technique, I was carrying back memories of Paris, glimpses of the boulevards and the fashionable shops, of the little sidewalk cafés with their striped awnings, of Napoleon's Tomb and the Tuilleries.

The world was very kind.  And I hugged my two billiard cues a little closer as the train gathered speed for Havre—and home.

# CHAPTER XVI

### A TOUR WITH JACOB SCHAEFER, THE WIZARD

It was Doctor Jennings, the Crescent Club amateur, who first suggested to Jacob Schaefer that he take me on tour as a playing partner. That was in January, 1903, shortly after I returned to America from my first trip to Paris. Schaefer, also under the ban of the French Government, had finished his engagement at the Grand Café and followed me within a few weeks.

Schaefer had complained that the first class American players, Morningstar, Sutton, and Slosson wanted too much for their services. By the time he had paid the salary they asked, he would have nothing left for himself.

"Why don't you grab this youngster for your exhibition tour, Jake," Doctor Jennings suggested. "He's still in short pants. You and he would make a great team on the road."

So Schaefer approached my father, and they made a deal. There were two reasons, my father explained to me, why such an arrangement would be favorable to us. In the first place it would eliminate the expense and worry of booking our own tour; and secondly, it would give me an opportunity to study under the greatest living master of the game.

It proved a mighty fine thing for me. I learned more billiards under Jacob Schaefer than in any similar period of my life.

He was not the teaching type. He would never volunteer any suggestions or stop to analyze his game for my benefit. But it was an inspiration simply to play with him, and watch his game from day to day.

Schaefer was a billiard genius. He played with his subconscious mind, in contradistinction to Vignaux, Ives and Morningstar, the intellectual type. He had the most delicate stroke in the world, and he seemed to have a better sense of the "feel" of ivory than any other billiard player.

At the table he was quick to size up a situation, and quick to execute. No slow processes of calculation for him. No walking around the table and squinting at the balls from various angles. He knew instinctively what to do, and he did it.

Once he had the balls under control, his game was beautiful to watch. He shot so rapidly that he was mentally two or three strokes ahead of his cue, all the time. Almost before the ball stopped rolling he was poised, delicately stroking his cue for the next shot.

Schaefer was a great "shot maker." That is, he had the all-round skill to execute the most difficult shot on the table. But his greatest stroke was the massé.

Early French players first discovered the massé. It was first demonstrated in America, according to Maurice Daly, by M. Berger. But as they developed it, it was merely a "crush" stroke. The cue descended upon the ball forcibly, and although the necessary sharp curve resulted, the object balls were scattered all over the table.

Schaefer changed all that. He brought his cue tip down as lightly as a feather, stroking the ivory with a touch that was almost a caress. No matter how sharp the angle, he could swing the ball around without too much force, and his massé shots left the balls always nicely placed.

In a match with a French expert at the Grand Café, Schaefer made one of the most remarkable massé shots I ever saw. The balls were lined up on the lower rail, six or eight inches apart, in the left hand balk, with the cue ball frozen to the side rail. Schaefer not only had to make the carom, but drive one of the object balls out of balk. He poised his cue for an instant, and then brought it down lightly and firmly. The cue ball shot out in a wide

## LIKE FATHER, LIKE SON

Jacob Schaefer, the famous old Wizard, imparting some of his billiard skill to Young Jake, who subsequently won the world's championship from Hoppe, only to hand it back again. Strangely enough the younger Schaefer's style is totally unlike the old Wizard's, but it is generally agreed that he plays a more finished, all-around game than his illustrious father.

curve, missing the first object ball completely. Everybody thought he had missed. The French player sprang from his chair and reached for the chalk. But Schaefer waved him back.

The cue ball turned in sharply, struck the further object ball, driving it out of balk, and then completed the carom along the rail to the red ball.

On another occasion I saw him play a massé shot the entire length of the table, calculating the break of the curve to the fraction of an inch. Not one billiard player could do that, if he practised all his life. It was sheer genius.

Schaefer was a little man, not over five feet five. But there was not a shot on the table he couldn't reach. He used to walk around the table like a little game cock, with his cue poised as lightly as a fencer's rapier. Using his right and left hands equally well, bending over, now on tip-toe, he would score his points almost as rapidly as the referee could count them.

In our exhibition matches he gave me plenty of opportunity to display my skill. Sometimes he would leave the balls favorably located, so that I could get off to a flying start. But when I got too far out in front, with a long run or two, he would settle down and play the best billiards he knew how, for he was very jealous of his laurels.

A street car accident in Chicago resulted in a

broken wrist, which gave Schaefer considerable trouble in later years. He was fond of his stimulants, too, and was not very careful about keeping in condition. He was so convinced of his own prowess, that he thought he could go into a match without practice or preparation, and beat any player in the world.

There came a time, however, when his careless, erratic manner of living told on him. In his last great match with Louis Cure, in France, they had to give him plentiful draughts of whiskey on the final night, to keep him going. He played the last hundred points on nerve alone, and when the last winning carom had been scored, he dropped down on the table with his head on the cloth, and his cue clattering to the floor. They had to carry him to his room in the hotel, and it was several days before he walked about and held a cue again.

# CHAPTER XVII

## THE HOPPE FAMILY MIGRATES TO PARIS

AFTER one season on the road with the Wizard, I received another offer to go to Paris. The difficulties with the government had been settled, temporarily, at least, and the Olympia wanted to engage me for a six months' stay, guaranteeing $32 a day, six days a week.

That was more than twice as much as I had received before. It did not take the Hoppe family long to reach a decision. On $32 a day all of us could live quite comfortably in Paris. So we packed up, and away we went.

My father took a house in the Rue Madeline, near the Kammerers' home, and before long we were comfortably established there. I had learned a few words of French on my previous visit, so I was the official guide for the family.

Every morning we used to take a long walk down the Champs Elysees. Then back to the Olympia in the Rue des Capucines, where my father would supervise an hour or two of strict practice. It seemed good to have him there at the edge of the table again, scolding me when I played too hastily, lecturing me sternly in German when the balls didn't roll right.

That year marked an epoch in my career. I bought my first pair of long trousers! No longer the "Boy Wonder" I couldn't scramble up on the table any more to play shots that were out of reach. But I had added a few inches to my height, and although I still avoided it whenever possible, I could use the bridge on shots that could not be reached any other way.

Six months more of practice under my father's watchful eye; six months of hard-fought exhibition matches with Vignaux, Cure, Morningstar, Fournil and others, balk line mingled with three cushions and red ball, and my game showed steady improvement.

I learned this about playing in the Paris academies. You become accustomed to the lights, the cushions and the cloth. The conditions are always the same and you don't have to readjust your stroke every time you come to the table. That explains, perhaps, why the French experts roll up such high averages and then fail when they come over here.

In America the professional has to travel about the country, playing on a different table nearly every night. And while our averages suffer, at times, on these long exhibition tours, it it better in the long run to develop a versatile, all-around game.

I made several runs of two hundred that winter, and I played nearly all my opponents on even terms. I was averaging between twenty and thirty at 18 inch balk line, two shots in.

Returning to the United States the following Spring, my father endeavored to obtain a match with George Slosson, who had recently beaten Schaefer for the 18.2 championship. But Mr. Slosson was wary.

"Who is this young man?" he inquired. "Whom has he beaten? Let him get a reputation and then come back. I cannot accept the challenge of an unknown."

You can well imagine what my father replied to that. But it did no good to argue the matter. At the age of 17, I was in no position to dictate terms to the world's champion. I had to be patient and bide my time.

With Schaefer as a partner I made another tour of the United States in the Spring of 1905. We played in most of the principal cities, and under his guidance I acquired still more billiard technique and inspiration.

In the fall of 1905, I made another unsuccessful attempt to challenge Slosson for a championship

match.  Failing in that, my father and I made preparations to go to Paris again.

But we were not bound for another season of exhibitions at the Olympia.  This time we were bent
on more serious business.  Maurice Vignaux had
beaten George Sutton in March, 1903, for the
world's championship at 18.1, and it was our intention to challenge him for the title.

After some preliminary negotiations by cable we
set sail for France in December.  M. Vignaux cor-
dially accepted my challenge.  Forfeits were posted,
the terms announced, and we settled down to prepare
for the match.

M. Vignaux conducted his daily practice sessions
at the Grand Café.  My father used to drop in
there, in the afternoons, to watch him.  Surrounded
by a coterie of enthusiastic admirers, the old fellow
radiated self confidence.  My father kept a careful
check on his practice averages, his best runs, and
noted carefully the shots he missed.

Meanwhile I kept to my old stamping ground,
the Olympia.  I practised faithfully two hours each
morning, and in the afternoon played an exhibition
at balk line with one or two opponents.  Most of
my efforts were concentrated on getting the "line,"
and nursing in the center panel.

I was confident, too.  But it would not do to
underestimate the old Lion of France.  He had

more than thirty years of playing experience behind him. His eye was keen; his hand steady. I had watched him play too often to regard him lightly as an antagonist.

Back in 1899 Maurice Daly had predicted that I would be World's Champion before I was out of my teens. Well, I was eighteen now.

# CHAPTER XVIII

## I CROSS CUES WITH THE OLD LION, VIGNAUX

THINK back across the years and see if you can remember the fifteenth of January, Nineteen hundred and six. For you, doubtless that day is faded and old and forgotten. But I shall never forget it. That fifteenth of January is as fresh and bright colored in my memory as any yesterday.

"Maurice Vignaux of France, billiard champion of the world versus Willie Hoppe of America, challenger; an international match of 500 points for the world's championship at 18.1, a purse of $1,000 and a diamond trophy; in the Grand Ball Room of the Grand Hotel tonight."

It rained that morning, and I slept late. My father would not let me touch my billiard cue. Instead of the two-hour practice session at the Olympia we went for a long walk down the Champs Elysees. Fresh air and exercise, a clear head and keen eyes for the match that night. So we strolled along through the drizzling rain, my father keeping up an incessant conversation to prevent me, I suspect, from brooding over impending events.

Back to the Boulevard des Capucines at noon. We climbed the stair to the Olympia Academy and sat in the gallery, watching Fournil and Sanchez, two short-stop professionals, ticking away at balk line. Occasionally, as I sat there watching the balls move back and forth, my mind leaped ahead to the big match that was to come. I was restless; on edge. I wanted to get my hands on my cue, to chalk it and sandpaper it, and file the leather tip. But my father wouldn't let me near a billiard table.

In the middle of the afternoon we went to dinner in a little restaurant around the corner in the Rue Scribe. At least, my father had dinner. All he ordered for me was some mutton broth and crackers. Billiard players, like athletes in every other branch of sport eat sparingly before competition. My father, who watched my diet as carefully as he watched my billiard stroke had calculated the dinner hour so that I would step to the table that night untroubled by an overworked digestion.

Then, when I had finished my meager meal and the waiter had cleared the table, my father lighted a cigar and began to give me final instructions for the match. What they were, I can't remember. But I recall how the waiter stood a little way off, with his serviette on his arm, watching my father draw intricate diagrams on the table cloth with the sharp edge of a spoon, and how he came closer and studied these diagrams over my father's shoulder, trying to solve the puzzle contained in the little circles and triangles, and how he finally gave up in despair, shrugged his shoulders and went away.

The stern lecture that went with these diagrams was even more involved. I must remember to keep the balls away from the corners; watch for a chance to get the "line"; never take any chances in driving them out of balk; play safety if nothing better offered.

I nodded. I had heard all that before. But my own campaign was much simpler and, I thought, more effective. Make billiards, and then make more billiards, and keep M. Vignaux sitting in his chair.

It was after 5 when we left the restaurant. My father took me to our room, tucked me in with a couple of blankets and told me to take a nap. Strangely enough, the long walk of the morning and the nervous tension of the day had brought a slight fatigue, and I fell asleep without difficulty.

My father's knock on the door wakened me at 7. And now, as I washed my face in cold water, and donned a fresh white shirt and dinner jacket, I was quite calm, and cool. The nerve strain had gone. At the Olympia, my father gave me my cue, and a set of ivory, and for twenty minutes or half an hour I knocked the balls around, just to limber up my stroke. Then, at the stroke of 8 we started for the scene of the match, a block and a half away.

A procession of carriages was rolling up to the main entrance of the Grand Hotel as we arrived, discharging a steady stream of men in opera hats and women in evening dress. There was Tod Sloan, the famous jockey, Nat Goodwin and Eddie Foy, all decked out in "soup-and-fish." Yonder in the lobby, surrounded by a group of admirers was the old Lion, Vignaux, himself. He was screwing the two sections of his cue together, making ready for the fray.

And now here comes the Comte de Dree, the official referee. He marches us into the ball room, where most of the spectators have already taken their seats, and makes a speech in French. I gather from his gestures which range from the crystal chandelier overhead to Eddie Foy, standing in the doorway, that this is indeed a momentous occasion. He waves his hand toward me. I stand and bow and there is a generous clapping of hands. He waves his hand toward the old Lion and the spectators rise to their feet with a roar.

The hubbub subsides; we bank for the break, and the game is on.

By a scant margin, I won the lag, counted the opening shot and made a run of 12. M. Vignaux

replied with 9.   In the third inning, playing with all
his old confidence he put together a run of 32, and
I came back in the fourth with 27.

For several innings we kept nearly on even terms.
Then in the eighth, Vignaux gathered the balls
skillfully and held them in control for a beautiful
cluster of 61.   Two innings later he added 30, and
in the thirteenth, 47.   In this run of 47 he made a
remarkable draw shot, three fourths of the length
of the table, gathering the balls perfectly for position in the lower balk.   As the balls came to position,
the crowd arose and cheered him, and the old Lion
had to rest his cue a moment and wait for the applause to subside.

Meanwhile I had been plugging along with indif-
ferent success, my best run being a 38 in the 11th
inning.

At the "half time" interval, when play was suspended fifteen minutes for the usual rest and
promenade, Vignaux was leading me 266 to 228.
In the French section they were offering thousands
of francs at 4 and 5 to 1 on Vignaux with few
takers.   My American supporters, who had already
wagered large sums on the outcome of the match,
strode up and down the lobby, diligently smoking
their cigars and looking extremely glum.

# CHAPTER XIX

## I STAGE A LATE RALLY

WHEN play was suspended at the half time interval, with Vignaux leading, 266 to my 228, the referee marked the position of the balls with a lead pencil and removed them from the table. This was to prevent any tampering, on the part of the spectators, with the "leave." As was the custom, the referee turned M. Vignaux's ball over to the second, handed mine to my father, and took charge of the red ball, himself.

My father placed my ball in his pocket as we started out for our walk in the lobby. This served to keep the ivory warm, for there is nothing more susceptible to a chilling draft than a billiard ball. It also made sure that no one could substitute an inferior ball for the finish of the game.

My father was curiously silent as we paced along. No scolding for lost opportunities; no reproach. A couple of telegraph instruments were clicking in a little room just off the lobby. The correspondent of the New York Herald was sending an early account of the match, and we stopped a moment to talk with him.

He told us that he had arranged a code system with the sporting editor of the Herald in New York whereby the billiard table was divided into hundreds of squares, like a checkerboard. With a set of symbols and numbers he could describe any shot made during the match, and the exact diagram would be reproduced in the newspaper the following morning.

"They have asked me to send a thousand words and half a dozen diagrams," he said.

We walked on. The click of the telegraph was telling America that Vignaux led me by 266 to 228.

We resumed play. The balls were restored to their position on the table; the spectators settled back in their seats. As I walked to the table I could still hear the faint chatter of the telegraph outside.

"Willie Hoppe loses" or "Willie Hoppe wins world's championship"—which message would the cables carry back home? But this was no time for sentimental reflections.

I made two and missed. Vignaux could collect only four. Then the balls began to respond to my touch. I gathered them on the line near the lower rail and ran 51, my highest cluster of the evening so

# I STAGE A LATE RALLY 95

far. I had passed Vignaux on my 41st carom and
now led him by 10 points.

The old Lion played slowly, carefully. I can still
see him rise from his chair with the shred of a
cigarette—which he rolled himself—hanging from
his lip. Majestically he chalks his cue and surveys
the table. There is a certain regal air about him as
he settles down for the stroke. He runs nine and
then—tragedy! He fails to drive them out of balk,
and sits down, reaching in his pocket for his tobacco
to console himself with another one of his tiny
cigarettes.

Score: Hoppe, 281; Vignaux, 279.

I add nine more to my string, and after Vignaux
has collected 7, I go to the table and gather 34, turn-
ing the third century with a fair margin. Nine more
for Vignaux, then a miss.

The balls are nicely placed. I play slowly at first,
then, as they respond perfectly to the touch, I let
myself out a little. I forget about the telegraph; I
forget the crowded boxes and the tiers of seats rising
around the ball room. These rows of faces are faint
and blurred and far away like strange fish seen
through the greenish waters of an aquarium. In the
stillness I am lost, sunk, abandoned at the bottom
of the sea with this abstract problem in shifting
ivory. The voice of the Comte de Dree, counting
the points . . . the click and whirr of the balls

. . . except for these, all the noises of Paris are hushed and the world has paused on its axis . . .

Ninety-three!

I go to my seat, drowned in a storm of applause for the highest run of the evening.

Vignaux is cold and stiff from sitting so long in his chair. He rises, chalks his cue with grim determination. An old Lion still—at bay. He settles down to the table . . . makes a long carom . . . misses . . .

A tired old man who feels his mantle slipping from his shoulders.

Score: Hoppe 417; Vignaux, 295.

After a short run of 8, collected in the open table, I miss. Vignaux steps again to the table. Every eye is upon him, for it is plain he is summoning all his old genius and strategy. While the crowd watches, breathless, he puts together a run of 27 caroms. His last stand.

Again the balls respond to my touch. I push resolutely ahead. Fifty-seven, with 26 more to go. The balls line up in the middle of the table. They are too wide for a massé. A kiss shot is out of the question. Without a pause to study the angle, I swing my cue boldly into the ball. It flies around the table—four cushions—and completes the count.

There is no stopping me now. I have the bit

Winning His First World's Championship—Willie Hoppe Banking for the Break in His Famous Match with Maurice Vignaux, January 15, 1906, in the Grand Ball Room of the Grand Hotel, Paris

between my teeth. Suddenly, above the monotonous drone of the referee's voice counting the points I hear a new note:

". . . et pour trois!"

I am very tired. My cue is strangely heavy. It swings mechanically and the ball counts.

". . . et pour deux!" Another carom successfully completed.

". . . et pour un!" A single, solitary carom stands between me and the billiard championship of the world. It has cost me a boy's inheritance.

". . . et gagner!"

I have made it.

I am drowned in a roar of triumph! I am caught up violently by enthusiastic Americans and swept around the table on their shoulders. Hats are tossed in the air, trampled under foot. Strange faces swirl around me. My father's voice, thick with wine and emotion: "Willie . . . Willie!" My back is thumped, my hand squeezed and my tired right arm wrung like a pump handle. Somebody starts to sing. It is Eddie Foy. Everybody is singing. The Star Spangled Banner. I am thinking, "so this is what it means to be champion."

Over the tossing heads of the throng I catch a glimpse of Vignaux. He is still sitting in his chair, a tired old man; the fingers that failed him, mechanically rolling a cigarette . . .

For those who are statistically minded I set down
the score:

Hoppe:

12   5   0 27   2 27 16 20   8   0 38 14 12
17 28   (half time)   2 51   9 34 93   8 75
—Total 500; average, 20 20-24.

Vignaux:

9   4 32 13   7   0   1 61   4 30   8   0
47   0 24 (half time) 4   9   7   9   1 27
—Total, 322; average, 14 1-23.

# CHAPTER XX

IT was long after midnight when my father and I walked slowly along the Rue des Capucines to our little hotel. Still in a daze, I heard him talking of the big things yet to come, of the thousands of dollars I would earn as world's champion. Perhaps he said, we would open a big billiard room in New York and all the country would flock there to see me give exhibitions.

Vignaux, he said, had made more than a million francs in the thirty years of his billiard supremacy. He had lived in grand style, mingled with a rich and famous sporting crowd, owned a string of race horses. Now, by virtue of my conquest in the Grand Hotel, all these things had descended to the Hoppe family.

I was thinking: "What a long, long journey from the little barber shop at Cornwall Landing."

When we reached our hotel room I emptied my pockets on the bed. Here was a crumpled $100

99

bill; a gold watch and chain; a bank note for a thousand francs; miscellaneous small bills and a dozen gold pieces—presents amounting to more than $1,000, chiefly from my backers who had won thousands on the match.

There was a diamond trophy, too; the emblem of the championship which my father had taken in charge. Altogether, with the purse and my share of the gate receipts I was $5,000 richer in immediate cash from that eventful night.

The next morning came a sheaf of cablegrams from America; congratulations, challenges, requests for exhibitions. Several newspapers wanted me to write an article about winning the championship.

My father bought a Paris edition of the New York Herald, and when he had read its enthusiastic account of the match, he bought all the Paris papers he could find and waded laboriously through the sporting columns, gleaning what fragmentary comment he could from the French idiom.

Paris, it seemed, was quite enthusiastic over my victory as if I had been a native son. One writer recalled how I had first made my appearance at the Olympia Academy five years before, a little boy in short trousers, and described the development of my game under Paris influences.

Everywhere I went—and my father took a good deal of pride in marching me down the Champs

Élysées and visiting all the sporting rendezvous—they shook me by the hand and showered me with congratulations.

We lingered only a few days in the French capital. On the way home we stopped at Antwerp, where I gave a three days exhibition. Then, with the billiard championship of the world, more money than I had ever possessed before, and stirring memories of that eventful night at the Grand Hotel, we took steamer for New York.

Big things were in store. No sooner had I landed in America than George Slosson challenged me for a championship match. He was the same Slosson who had inquired who I was, and advised me to "get a reputation" when I had challenged him the year before. Now it was my turn.

My father accepted his challenge readily. The stakes were posted and arrangements made for a match in Grand Central Palace on March 28.

In the interval of preparation I made my headquarters in New York and learned what an extraordinary thing it is to be a world's champion. I was besieged by reporters. In spite of the complete reports that had been sent over on the match with Vignaux, they all wanted to learn the story from me, and I had to give my own version of the match a score of times.

I was photographed in every conceivable posture

around a billiard table, with my cue at all angles. Dinners were given in my honor at half a dozen clubs, and the requests for exhibitions were so numerous that my father had to hire a secretary to answer the mail.

Was I bored by all this flattery? Not a bit of it. I was having the time of my young life. It had been a tough climb to the top and I thoroughly enjoyed the sensation of being a large frog in the billiard pond. If I hadn't, I'd have been less than human.

The sporting pages were filled with my coming match with Slosson. Opinion was divided. Slosson's supporters pointed out that I had won my championship from an old man, just barely able to totter around the table; that anybody could have beaten Vignaux that night at the Grand Hotel. They overlooked the fact that I had finished the last half of the game with an average of forty, and had made a grand average of approximately 21, which, at 18.1 is a creditable performance against any opponent.

Slosson himself was confident. He had seen me as a youngster in short trousers, and he still considered me at the "Boy Wonder" stage, when I used to lie at full length on the table and bounce off on the floor.

So lively was the interest that all tickets to the

Grand Central Palace were sold out nearly a week
before the match. When the night finally came,
speculators out in Lexington Avenue were selling
seats at $30 and $40 a pair.

It was the largest crowd that ever saw a billiard
match in the United States, perhaps in all the world.
Including the standees, more than four thousand per-
sons were present.

I was nervous and so was Slosson. The conditions were not the best. The size of the restless
crowd, the strain of my new-won laurels, the very
hugeness of Grand Central Palace itself conspired
to make the match tedious and slow. Then, too,
there was another mental hazard for upstairs in one
of the balcony boxes sat my mother and sisters, and
despite their pride and enthusiasm, I didn't feel quite
at ease.

But I won. After a slow start, during which
Slosson forged ahead with an early run of 61, I
came along steadily and finished with a comfortable
margin, 500 to 391 in 46 innings for the unhappy
average of 10 40-46. Slosson's average was 8 31-45
and his high runs 61, 53 and 30; while I had three
clusters of 56, 45 and 42.

Let me observe here that 18.1—the style of game
we were playing then—is far more difficult than
18.2, the popular game today. In 18.2 you have
always a preliminary shot in balk, to maneuver the

balls over the line on your next carom. The value of that first shot in is incalculable. It enables you to plan your campaign at close range, so to speak. But in 18.1 there is no close manipulation in balk. Out they must go on the first shot.

The comparison of the two styles of balk-line is clearly shown in the records. For many years the world's record high run at 18.1 (in actual championship competition) has stood at 140, whereas at 18.2 runs of more than two hundred are common in every championship tournament. Welker Cochran holds the world's record at present with a run of 384, made in a game against George Sutton in Chicago in November, 1921. That run is all the more remarkable when it is considered it was made in a game of 400 points.

It appears difficult to understand how my game could have fallen off 50 per cent from the match in Paris, January 15, when I averaged approximately 21, to the match with Slosson, March 28, when my average was only a fraction above 10. Yet such are the vagaries of billiards.

Those three ivory balls are not always tame and obedient. Just because you have conquered them once don't think you have subdued them for all time. Ivory is not such servile stuff. The game of billiards always demands the best you have of concentration and control.

# CHAPTER XXI

## MY FIRST TOURNAMENT FOR THE WORLD'S CHAMPIONSHIP AT 18.2

CLOSE on the heels of the challenge match with George Slosson at Grand Central Palace the night of March 28, 1906 came a tournament for the world's championship at 18.2. It, too, was held in New York City, in the Concert Hall of Madison Square Garden and all the great experts of the world, with the exception of Maurice Vignaux, were entered.

Although I was very modest about it, I expected this tournament to be duck soup for me. Had I not bearded the Great Lion, Vignaux in his den in Paris? Had I not conquered The Student in New York before the greatest crowd that ever witnessed a billiard match?

At the age of 18, these were convincing reasons why I should romp through the field and add the 18.2 championship to my laurels. But not so fast, Willie. Ivory is a fickle mistress and these old-timers, Schaefer, and Sutton and Slosson have yet a trick or two up their sleeves.

After the match with Sutton I had a scant two weeks to change my game from 18.1 to 18.2. My practice sessions were all devoted to close manipulation, massés, and delicate nursing in the short table, and when the tournament started on April 9, I was supremely confident.

I started off auspiciously, defeating Albert Cutler, the young Boston professional 500 to 382, with an average a fraction better than twenty. In my next game I encountered Ora Morningstar, the Western expert, who was said to have inherited the theories, style and strategy of the late Frank Ives. I won that game, too, but not without passing through one of the strangest ordeals ever encountered at a billiard table.

Along toward the middle of the game, with the balls rolling nicely in my favor, I found myself, near the side rail, confronted with a massé shot. I raised my cue and took the stance, only to find that a fly, a common house fly, had alighted on the cue ball at exactly the spot I wanted to hit.

I paused a second, waiting for him to go away. He didn't budge. The referee came close and took out his handkerchief, shooing the fly away. Again I lifted my cue. Back came the fly and settled down once more in the same spot. Once again

the referee shooed away, and once again he circled
around and came back again to his old perch.

The spectators were laughing. Those nearest
the table joined in the sport. They waved hats,
newspapers, score cards and umbrellas in a series
of threatening gestures that would have frightened
an elephant, and each time, when the commotion
subsided, the fly came back and sat down on the
exact spot where I wanted to hit the ball.

Charlie Somerville, the short story writer, who
was then a reporter on a New York newspaper says
he counted 18 distinct times I raised my cue to
shoot, only to be thwarted each time by the returning fly. The only satisfactory explanation I ever
heard for the episode was this: the fly had run across
a grain of sugar or chalk on the ball, and he was
determined to finish the tidbit in spite of our billiard
game.

At last somebody killed him. I wish I had his
small carcass preserved in alcohol. He was the most
splendid example of tenacity I ever saw.

When at length the tumult and laughing died out
and I raised my cue the nineteenth time, I found
all my powers of concentration gone. I missed the
proverbial mile. The wonder is that I won the
game at all, but I had little opposition from Morningstar, and won, 500 to 207.

George Slosson had his revenge when we met in

the eleventh game of the tournament.   He beat me 500 to 245 with an average of 20.83 to my 10.65. It was a clear cut victory, and I have no alibi.

Then came a famous, record-breaking match with George Butler Sutton.   Sutton had developed the line nurse, and the drive and block system of balk-line scoring further than any professional at that time, although his all-round execution was not as effective as Slosson's or Schaefer's.   In this particular match, the balls rolled perfectly to his delicate stroke, and he gave a marvelous exhibition.

Inasmuch as that game is still a world's record for 500 point competition, I am going to give the score in detail.   I won the bank, made the opening shot and ran 11, leaving them in close position. Sutton controlled them nicely for a run of 128. Back I came with 50, and he replied with 14.   In my third trip to the table I accumulated 53 more. Score, Sutton 142, Hoppe, 114.

Two goose eggs followed, one apiece, and then Sutton got his line nurse working perfectly again for a run of 124.   I could score only 4 from the leave and I sat down.   I was destined to sit in my chair for the rest of the game.   With that delicate, edging stroke of his Sutton ran out his string with an unfinished run of 234.   Along toward the end of this last run, when it appeared that I had no more chance of winning I found myself "rooting" for

Sutton as enthusiastically as anybody in the house.
I wanted him to go ahead and hang up that marvelous average of 100.

There is another side-light about the game of
billiards. More than any other game I know of it
brings out qualities of sportsmanship and appreciation of your opponent's fine game.

Here is the summary of that notable encounter:

Sutton—128, 14, 0, 124, 234—500 Average, 100
Hoppe—11, 50, 53, 0, 4—118 Average 23.2.

It was along in the second inning of that game,
while I was at the table that I became aware of a
sudden outburst of enthusiasm from the audience.
Now there are two occasions when a billiard audience always applauds: when you pull off some
circus shot, or when you reach 100. I had performed neither of these feats, and yet the audience
had burst into a thunder of enthusiasm.

I stopped playing and looked up. Coming in at
the door was a majestic figure of a man with a huge
shock of white hair. It was Mark Twain, one of
the most enthusiastic billiard fans I ever knew. In
the next chapter I shall try to give some glimpses
of Mark Twain at the billiard table, and repeat the
billiard story he told us that night at Madison Square
Garden.

# CHAPTER XXII

## MARK TWAIN, A GREAT OLD BILLIARD FAN

WHEN the game with Sutton was ended, and the crowd had finished its enthusiastic demonstration over his marvelous performance in averaging 100, the referee held up his hand for silence.

"We have a distinguished visitor with us here tonight," he said, waving his hand toward Mark Twain. "You all know him and love him. I've seen him at every big billiard match in New York for years. Let's see if we can't get him to say a few words on this memorable occasion."

Twain stood up, and all the audience settled back in their seats. He congratulated Sutton on his remarkable performance, and then turned and congratulated me on holding my cue so steadfastly during my long tenure in the chair. Then he told a story.

"Once in Nevada," he began, "I dropped into a billiard room casually and picked up a cue and began to knock the balls around. The proprietor, who was a red-haired man, with such hair as I have never seen anywhere except on a torch, asked me if I would like to play. I said 'Yes.' He said, 'Knock the balls around a little and let me see how you can shoot.' So I knocked them around and thought I was doing pretty well when he said, 'That's all right, I'll play you left handed.' It hurt my pride but I played him. We banked for the shot and he won it. Then he commenced to play, and I commenced to chalk my cue to get ready to play and he went on playing, and I went on chalking my cue; and he played and I chalked all through the game. When he had run his string out I said:

" 'That's wonderful! Perfectly wonderful! If you can play that way left handed, what could you do right handed?'

" 'Couldn't do anything,' he said, 'I'm a left handed man.' "

I cherish a copy of Mark Twain's biography, in which Albert Bigelow Paine, his biographer says Twain " had great admiration for the young champion, Hoppe, because of his youth and his brilliant skill."

I am indebted also to the biographer for some interesting glimpses of Twain playing billiards in his own home, at No. 21 Fifth Avenue. With his usual impulsiveness, Twain, it seems had suddenly planned, in November of 1906 to make a trip to

Egypt. He had booked passage on a steamer and engaged a travelling secretary, intending to spend the remainder of the Winter up the Nile.

About that time the late H. H. Rogers, Standard Oil executive and a great friend of Twain's, let it become known that he and Mrs. Rogers intended giving the author a billiard table for Christmas. The news delighted Twain so that he couldn't wait and he suggested tactfully that the gift would be acceptable "right now." So he and Mr. Rogers paid a visit to the Brunswick-Balke-Collender Company and Twain picked out a handsome combination table, completely equipped with balls, racks, cues, etc., the best that money could buy.

He moved his bed from the bed room into the library to make room for the table, and when it was installed, he was as happy as a child over a new toy. He told Paine:

"I am not going to Egypt. There was a man here yesterday who said it was bad for bronchitis and, besides it's too far away from this billiard table." So he cancelled his passage, released the travelling secretary and settled down to spend the winter at home.

Acknowledging the gift, in a letter to Mrs. Rogers he wrote:

"Dear Mrs. Rogers:

"The billiard table is better than the doctors. I

## "What D'Ye Do in a Case Like This?"

Mark Twain, an enthusiastic follower of Hoppe's career, spent five or six hours a day around his own billiard table, and acquired considerable skill with the cue.

have a billiardist on the premises and walk not less than ten miles every day with my cue in my hand. And the walking is not the whole of the exercise, nor the most health-giving part of it, I think. Through the multitude of positions and attitudes it brings into play every muscle in the body and exercises them all.

"The games begin right after luncheons, daily, and continue until midnight, with 2 hours intermission for dinner and music. And so it is 9 hours exercise per day and 10 or 12 on Sunday. Yesterday and last night it was 12—and I slept until 8 this morning without waking.

"The billiard table as a Sabbath breaker can beat any coal-breaker in Pennsylvania, and give it 30 in the game. If Mr. Rogers will take to daily billiards he can do without the doctors and the massageur, I think.

"With Love and Many thanks,

"S. L. C."

Paine says that Mark Twain was forever inventing new games and making new rules for the old ones on the billiard table. Chiefly, however, he played the English game, which combines caroms and pockets, and widens the scope of scoring possibilities.

He took his billiards very seriously, too. Whenever a distinguished guest would drop in at 21 Fifth

Avenue, Twain would lead him as quickly as possible to the billiard room and try him out there. Col. George Harvey, then editor of the *North American Review,* and Finley Peter Dunne (Mr. Dooley) were frequent contestants in Twain's billiard room.

But my own glimpses of him were obtained chiefly at championship matches. He attended them all. He used to come with H. H. Rogers and they would sit together in great arm chairs near the edge of the table, intent on every shot. What a figure he made, with his fine head of white hair and keen eyes!

Frank Ives used to boast that he had played before a great Maharajah in India. Many of the French nobility used to attend the matches in Paris in which Vignaux played. I have never had the good fortune to play before "the crowned heads of Europe," as Mr. Barnum used to phrase it, but I like to remember those old nights at Madison Square Garden when Mark Twain, with his halo of white hair sat grandly in an arm chair near the table and watched me play.

# CHAPTER XXIII

## SOME FAMOUS BILLIARD PERSONALITIES

BILLIARDS has been the chief diversion of some of the world's most famous characters. Napoleon, according to the historians, was devoted to the game. With Josephine as a partner he is said to have passed many hours in the billiard room at Versailles, and made it a popular recreation among the French court.

The origin of the game is obscure, but the most authentic records indicate that it was played about the time of the Crusades and the supposition is that the Crusaders picked it up on their long journeys and brought it back to Europe. Certainly billiards is older than golf or tennis, and baseball, compared to it, is in its infancy.

In my thirty years playing experience, I have come in contact with a number of billiard-playing celebrities.

Eddie Foy, the comedian, is probably the best known figure on the American stage who is identified with the game. He has been playing billiards as long, if not longer, than I have. He claims two distinctions, one, that he was the first person to bring blue chalk over to this country from France, and second, that he once beat me a game of three cushions 15 points to nothing!

Eddie used to commute pretty regularly between New York and Paris, in the old days. At that time, in the nineties, the only chalk used in this country was common white chalk. In France the manufacturers had hit upon a formula for a new blue billiard chalk, much like that in use today, which would greatly assist the leather tip in clinging to the ivory.

Playing in a Paris Academy one day, Eddie conceived the brilliant idea of importing some of this blue chalk—about a pocketful—to this country. For the next few weeks, every time he played a game of billiards in Paris, he walked out with the little blue squares in his coat pockets, until, by the time he was ready to sail, he had quite a little collection of the stuff.

The first day on his arrival in New York he strolled importantly into Daly's Academy, prepared to spring his fancy chalk on the boys. But after he had gathered a little crowd around and was about to demonstrate the merits of his discovery, he felt in all his pockets, and the chalk was gone.

Eddie left Daly's in a great hurry and went straight home.

"Mother," he shouted, "have you seen anything of some little blue squares of chalk I had in my coat pockets?"

Mrs. Foy pondered.

"Sure and is that what it was?" she said. "I thought they were some special kind of moth balls ye had to keep your clothes safe on the voyage. I threw them out in the alley this morning." Eddie hastily repaired to the alley and there rescued his precious chalk from the bottom of an ash can. Later he succeeded in demonstrating his new chalk so effectively to the boys up at Daly's that they were offering him $10 a cake for the stuff. As a matter of fact, the blue chalk was vastly superior to the white chalk then in use and it wasn't long before it was manufactured over here.

There are more than a score of billiard enthusiasts in Congress, and every time I play an exhibition in Washington there is sure to be a sprinkling of Senators and Representatives scattered through the audience. Probably the most consistent billiard fan in the capital is Nicholas Longworth, the Republican leader in the House. Like Mark Twain, he can be depended on to attend every important billiard exhibition, but unlike Twain, he has no great shock of white hair to decorate the table side. In fact, Mr. Longworth's head is remarkable for its resemblance to the white cue ball. But he is a good scout, and a first class billiard player, anyway.

Clarence Whitehill of the Metropolitan Opera Company, probably the world's greatest baritone in Wagnerian rôles plays billiards every day during the opera season at Jack Doyle's academy, which is nearly across the street from the Opera House. Whitehill told me once that after a hard morning's rehearsal, with all its trials and tribulations, there was nothing like an hour or two of billiards in the afternoon to put him on edge for the exacting performance of Parsifal or Lohengrin at night.

Paderewski, the great Polish pianist plays billiards frequently just before a concert. He says it is just the thing for limbering up his wrists and fingers. I once told him that it was his relaxed mind that benefitted more than wrists or fingers.

Perhaps, just to return the compliment, I ought to try playing the piano just before some of my championship balk line matches.

In the sporting world, billiard players are plentiful. Babe Ruth wields a wicked cue at the pocket game. John Kling, the old time catcher of the Chicago Cubs held the world's championship at pocket billiards back in 1909 or 1910. He is an expert at three cushions and balk line too. I have often seen him run 75 to 100 at 18.2. That is remarkable when you consider that Kling's fingers and wrists had to handle the pitching of Overall and Brown and all the rest of the old Cub pitchers for more than ten years. In spite of the battering his hands must have received, Kling is still able to handle a cue as well as the second rate professionals.

Jim Corbett is another sporting celebrity who finds relaxation in billiards. But the list is too long to attempt enumeration.

In a subsequent chapter I shall tell of a trip to the White House, where I played an exhibition before President Taft and his cabinet.

# CHAPTER XXIV

## SOME BALK LINE HISTORY

THE tournament held at Madison Square Garden in April, 1906, for the world's championship at 18.2 was the first of a memorable series. It was important in my own career, too, for it brought me in competition with the greatest masters of the game. I tried hard to win it, for it was my father's ambition that I should hold all major billiard championships at the age of 18. But I lost three games and finished fourth.

Going over those scores I find some measure of consolation in the fact that Sutton, in beating me, made a world's record average of 100, which is still unbroken for a match of 500 points.

Figures are always interesting. Here is a summary of my six matches in my first world's championship tournament:

Hoppe, 500; Cutler, 382. Winner's average, 20.83; loser's 16.6. Best runs, Hoppe, 68; Cutler, 60.

Hoppe, 500; Morningstar, 207. Winner's average, 20.83; loser's, 7.96. Best runs, Hoppe, 105; Morningstar, 37.

Slosson, 500; Hoppe 245. Winner's average, 20.83; loser's 10.65. Best runs, Slosson, 84; Hoppe, 56.

Sutton, 500; Hoppe, 118. Winner's average 100; loser's 23.2. Best runs, Sutton, 234; Hoppe, 53.

Hoppe, 500; Cure 336. Winner's average, 27.77; loser's, 18.66. Best runs, Hoppe 177; Cure 86.

Schaefer, 500; Hoppe, 448. Winner's average, 25; loser's, 25.68. Best runs Schaefer, 117; Hoppe, 145.

George Slosson won the championship with a score of 5 games won and 1 lost, losing only to Sutton. Sutton and Schaefer finished in a tie for second place, each having won 4 and lost 2 games. Sutton won the playoff, defeating Schaefer 500 to 287.

You will observe from these figures that I lost the two "hard luck" games of the tournament; one in which my opponent (Sutton) beat me with the phenomenal average of 100, and the other in which my opponent (Schaefer) beat me with an average lower than my own. It sometimes happens, in a close game that the loser, who has had one inning less than the winner, finishes with a higher average.

Studying over the figures of that tournament I find that George Slosson, the winner, finished with a grand average of 18.47 and a high run of 153; while my own grand average was two points better, 20.44 and my high run, 177.

These figures may be consoling, but they don't alter the fact that my high hopes of winning the 18.2 balk line crown the same year I had beaten Vignaux and Slosson at 18.1 were sadly dashed. Perhaps the three lickings I got at Madison Square Garden that April was the best thing that ever happened to me. At any rate, I was soon to have my revenge.

At the close of the tournament all the billiard experts with the exception of Cutler and Morningstar packed their cues and other paraphernalia and hurried out to Chicago where another tournament, with no championship at stake, was staged. I won this tournament without the loss of a single game, making a new high run of 307 which was destined to stand as a record in this country for many years.

Early the following fall George Sutton challenged Slosson and they played a 500 point match for the title at Madison Square Garden, October 18, 1906. Sutton won, 500 to 375 with the splendid average of 31.25 to Slosson's 25, and a high run of 202 to Slosson's 75.

Schaefer was next in line to challenge for the championship, but his health had failed completely that summer, and he had gone to Denver to rest.

So it was my turn. My challenge was accepted, forfeits posted, and Sutton and I met in Grand Central Palace the night of December 18, 1906. Sutton beat me nearly two to 1, making 500 to my 258, with an average of 26.31 to my 14.33.

Sutton at that time was at the height of his career, playing consistently better billiards than anybody else in the world. He was destined to hold the championship for nearly two years more, defending it successfully against Orlando Morningstar at Orchestra Hall, Chicago, in January, 1907 by the score of 500 to 472, and against Schaefer at the same place the following November, winning 500 to 241.

Tuberculosis had made such inroads in Schaefer's health that he was no longer the old wizard with the cue, and Sutton, playing fine billiards, beat him more than two to one, registering a splendid run of 232 and an average of 33.33.

And now we come to one of the freak matches in billiard history, in which all world's records were broken. But they were low records, not high ones. Morningstar challenged Sutton for a championship match in the winter of 1907-8, and they met in New York City at Lenox Lyceum January 27, 1908.

It was a bitter cold night, but in spite of the weather, a fair sized crowd turned out. There was a good deal of interest in the match, for Morningstar had been playing fine billiards in practice, and a good many followers of the game expected to see him win the championship that Sutton had held for nearly two years.

The janitor of the Lenox Lyceum was not at all interested, it seems, in billiards. Shortly after the match began, he banked his fires, turned off the heat, and went home. The temperature began to drop, slowly, at first, and then more rapidly as the icy wind began to creep in at the windows.

The ivory balls turned to pieces of stone. They lost all life and resiliency. The players too, became chilled. Between innings they kept their hands in their pockets, and blew on their fingers just before their turn to shoot.

It was impossible for either Morningstar or Sutton to play good billiards under such conditions. You couldn't draw a ball softly, or make a massé shot, or keep them in any semblance of control. It was long after midnight when Sutton finally ran his string out, winning by a score of 500 to Morningstar's 309. Sutton's average was 7.46 and Morningstar's, 4.68, while the respective high runs were 93 and 26.

So far as I know they are the lowest averages made in a championship match since the days of old Michael Phelan, when they played without any balk lines on the table, and nothing was barred.

# CHAPTER XXV

## I WIN THE WORLD'S CHAMPIONSHIP AT 18.2

My turn to challenge Sutton for his title came
again in March, 1908. The match was arranged
for Madison Square Garden the night of March
27, and the terms called for a side bet of $1,000,
with 60 per cent of the gate to go to the winner and
40 per cent to the loser.

During the era of prosperity that followed my
match with Vignaux, two years before, the Hoppe
family had accumulated enough to open a very re-
spectable billiard room in downtown Brooklyn. I
had made a number of profitable tours on the road,
but most of my playing had been in the Metropolitan District.

Now, in preparation for my forthcoming match,
I settled down to five hours practice daily in the
Brooklyn Billiard academy. My father was there
to keep an eye on me, and once again, whenever I
felt the youthful impulse to be careless or haphazard

in my execution, I heard an outraged explosion of parental wrath. It was time, my father told me, that I won the 18.2 championship. There must be no more monkey-business.

That night in Madison Square Garden I caught Sutton in a slump. I got the jump on him, played a steady consistent game, and although my average was not impressive, I left him far behind. A run of 99 in the ninth inning put me well in the lead, although he threatened to overtake me with a well played 83 in his 13th inning.

For the most part I played open billiards. I was resolved not to give him any more chances than necessary to get the balls on the line and employ his famous nurse system.

In the latter part of the game, I played more consistently, making 7 double figure runs in the last nine innings for a total of 188. I should have run out in the 23rd inning, but I played an around-the-table shot too hastily, and missed by a hair. I was so far ahead then, that it didn't make a great deal of difference, and I ran out my string of 500 in the next inning with a cluster of 5.

By a curious coincidence I had made my 500 points against Sutton in exactly the same number of innings required in the match against Vignaux. Consequently the averages were the same, 20, 20-24.

Here is the score of my first world's championship victory at 18.2:

Hoppe: 1 30 8 1 1 0 10 12 99 5 10 36 88 6 0 22 25 14 24 29 0 42 32 5—500. Average, 20, 20-24.

Sutton: 0 7 2 0 0 1 20 0 28 0 54 2 83 0 16 9 6 11 1 6 0 7 19 0—272. Average, 11, 8-24.

I now held, at the age of 20 years and 5 months and a half, all the recognized balk line championships. (The 14.2 championship, which I annexed a little later, was already becoming obsolete as a professional test, and has now passed entirely out of existence.)

Lest the reader think that I am inclined to boast unduly at this achievement, I should like at this opportunity to make a little digression, and give my own notion of the reasons underlying my triumph.

In the first place, I was not endowed with any heaven-sent gift for billiards. I had not been equipped, as a child, with any special set of muscles and nerves which enabled me to control billiard balls more successfully than the ordinary individual. I was not a "genius" in the sense that I had an abnormal brain, and an infinite capacity for taking pains.

To none of these things do I attribute my rise to

billiard fame and fortune. The whole thing in a nutshell is this :

My father, back in the Cornwall days, had taught me *not to miss!* There was a very definite penalty hanging over my head every time I took aim at the billiard balls. It was a question of making the shot and making it right, or finding myself sprawling across the room from a box on the ear. He was a stern, strict parent. There was no gentleness or sympathy in his make-up.

He instilled in my mind, from the earliest childhood practice sessions, a horror of missing. I didn't want to be bruised and beaten any more than I could help, so I kept my mind on the job. The result was natural, inevitable. I built up a billiard instinct, that was second nature.

In later years my father and I often disagreed. He advised me badly, I am afraid, in some of our negotiations after I had risen to the top. But all those differences and misunderstandings are wiped out and forgotten. For it is due to his discipline and his rigorous training that I won my billiard laurels. Another lad, blessed with such a persistent and single-purposed parent, might have done the same.

Thanks to my father, I had risen to the top. Whether I could stay there, I realized, depended solely on myself.

# CHAPTER XXVI

### GOLDEN DAYS!

PROSPERITY! Fame!

Gone the old days of struggle and hardship. Gone the barn-storming one-night stands in the sticks. World's champion at both 18.1 and 18.2, I could now command $50 or $100 every time I chalked my cue.

Leaving New York immediately after winning the title from George Sutton, I played a series of exhibition matches through the East with Schaefer, the Wizard. We drew capacity houses everywhere. For a 400 point exhibition the average fee I received was $50. That meant twelve and one half cents for every single point I made. In Philadelphia our receipts were more than $1,000 for a week of exhibitions.

This era of prosperity doubtless encouraged my father to adopt an independent attitude toward the world in general and the benevolent billiard trust, in particular. After holding the championship emblem only two weeks, I turned it back to the company, announcing that I would not defend it unless the conditions were changed.  What we asked was a three nights' match of 1,500 points, instead of the short 500 point match then in vogue.

The real reason for my break with the company was this; my father wanted to go into the manufacturing end of the business.  He had had several controversies with the company, over expenses on my trip to Paris, salary, etc., and now he was determined to form a new alliance, and go into the billiard business on a large scale.  So I resigned my championship, turned in the trophy, and became an "outlaw."

As a consequence, when the next tournament for the world's championship at 18.2 was held at Madison Square Garden in March and April, 1909, I was not among those present.  There was another conspicuous absence, too.  The Wizard, whose inspired cue had played a prominent part in every big billiard tournament for the last quarter of a century, had died of tuberculosis in Denver.

There were two newcomers in this event, both of whom were later to give a good account of themselves in the billiard world, Harry P. Cline and Calvin Demarest.  Slosson and Sutton, the two veterans, Morningstar, Cutler and Cure, the Frenchman, were the other contestants.

Morningstar won the tournament without the

loss of a single game. He, too, developed temperamental differences with the Brunswick-Balke-Collender Company and declined to defend the trophy on the terms they stipulated, joining me in the "outlaw" ranks.

With the two leading contenders barred from competition, another tournament was held at Madison Square Garden Concert Hall, November 22 to 29, 1909. In this event, professional billiards reached its low ebb in the United States. Although Firmin Cassignol, one of the leading French players, was imported to give an international flavor to the affair, the tournament was not a popular success. Demarest won it with an average of 15.35 after a three cornered tie with Sutton and Cline.

Demarest's reign was short. He held the balk line crown only two months, from December 2 to February 3, 1910, when he was defeated in a challenge match by Harry Cline, 1,500 to 1,387. This match, it will be noted, was played in three blocks of 500 points each, in accordance with the suggestion I made when I won the championship in 1908.

Cline was monarch of all he surveyed through February, March, April and a good part of May. In April, at Rex Hall in St. Louis, he administered a crushing defeat to Albert G. Cutler, 500 points to 42.

In the meantime my differences with the billiard

company had been ironed out. I was tired of exhibition work, however lucrative, and eager to get back into the competitive field. My friends, the sporting editors and writers on a number of newspapers had repeatedly called attention to the fact that the billiard title being handed about was an empty honor because I had never had a crack at it, and I was anxious to confirm their good opinion of me.

Accordingly, late in the spring of 1910 I challenged Harry Cline for his championship. The match was scheduled for the New York Theater Concert Hall, May 26, and once again I settled down to hard training. There is nothing like the thrill of approaching battle. Billiards in the abstract is a great game, but its interest is magnified ten fold when you have a hard tussle with a worthy opponent on your hands.

So it was, that after two years of travelling exhibitions "on my own," I chalked my cue against Harry Cline for the world's championship the night of May 26. There around the table sat all the old timers, welcoming me back again with noisy approval. There the lights, the crowd, the formal speech by the referee, the brand new table with its glistening cloth, my father sitting proudly in his chair with a huge cigar in his mouth, waiting to see son Willie do his stuff.

Well, to make a long story short, I beat him. The score was 500 to 394, and I averaged 17.85 to his 14.59. Not a very distinguished performance, but, as one of Mr. Shakespeare's characters once remarked, " . . . not as deep as a well nor as wide as a church door, but 'tis enough."

I was back in the billiard high chair once more. And this time I was destined to sit there, through storm and strife, for thirteen consecutive years.

# CHAPTER XXVII

### I PLAY AT THE WHITE HOUSE BEFORE PRES-
### IDENT TAFT AND HIS CABINET

"WILLIE," said my father, handing me a letter one day, soon after I had won the world's championship at 18.2 from Harry Cline, "read that." I opened the envelope and read—an invitation to play billiards at the White House before President Taft!

Well, in the long stretch of years since the Cornwall Landing days I had swung my cue in many places, from Parson Davies' New Orleans gambling house to the Grand Hotel in Paris, but I had never dreamed that the day would come when I would play in the White House before the President. And yet, why not? Other champions had displayed their skill under similar circumstances. Frank Ives had often boasted of spending two weeks with a celebrated Prince of India, teaching him the fine points of the English game. And in London it was no uncommon occurrence for the great professionals to play before the King or the Crown Prince.

Still I didn't know exactly how to go about training for it. I went to Maurice Daly, who knows all about formal affairs, for advice. Would I have to make a speech, and if so, what should I say?

Mr. Daly said:

"Pshaw; don't worry, Willie. Make the ivories do the talking. Show them the massé and the rail nurse."

Before the day arrived I spent several hours practicing fancy shots I had recently used in a vaudeville tour. The same billiard table on which I had recently won my championship at Madison Square Garden, an elaborate affair inlaid with ivory and ebony, was shipped to Washington and set up in the East Room.

President Taft had as his guests that night all the members of his cabinet and their families, and quite a few of the diplomatic corps. I was introduced all around and they made me feel quite at home.

"Pop" Daly had given me good advice. I made the ivories do the talking and the conversation never lagged. They had canvassed the diplomatic corps for some one adept at the game to cross cues with me. Failing to find an opponent there, Nicholas Longworth, representative from Ohio was chosen. We were to play a match of 100 points. Although he tried valiantly, the balls wouldn't perform satisfactorily for him and Mr. Longworth spent most of his time in his chair, watching me shoot. The score was 100 to 8.

I gave a short exhibition of balk line, then put them on the rail and somebody held a watch while I started out to make a run. It took a little less than five minutes to make 100 points.

President Taft and his cabinet officers were just as enthusiastic in their applause as any old time audience of fans in Madison Square Garden. Later I made some fancy shots, and showed them the principle of the massé.

After it was over we all had coffee, and several of the guests asked me to show them "how I did it." One of them looked gravely up my sleeve to see if I had any concealed wires or trick apparatus concealed there, while another accused me of having magic chalk, because I had made some thirty-five massé shots without a miss.

Altogether, it was a very lively party. When it was over I asked the President for an autographed photograph, which he gave me, together with a very cordial invitation to come back again.

I learned, incidentally, that President George Washington had established a billiard precedent in the executive mansion, and that he was fairly expert at the English game. My impression is that nearly all the presidents have spent considerable time in the White House billiard room.

CONCENTRATION IS THE KEYNOTE OF HOPPE'S GAME

Observe the workmanlike manner in which he bends over the rail to bring eye and brain to a sharp focus on the ball.

Not long after that I was called on to defend my billiard title again. Sutton had challenged, and the match was played at Madison Square Garden Concert Hall the night of November 28, 1911. The old expert of the nursing system only got the balls under good control once during the evening. On that occasion he made a nice run of 124. But my all around open table play was too much for him, and he succumbed by the score of 500 to 266. My winning average was 22.72, while his was only 12.09.

No other matches appeared in sight that winter. Meanwhile reports had come over from France of Louis Cure's great performances in Paris. He had been making runs of 200 and 300 with great regularity, it seemed, and the Paris academies were eager to stage another series of matches.

The invitation was alluring. The boulevards and the little cafés along the Rue Scribe held many pleasant memories. Paris beckoned. I packed my cues, said farewell to New York for a brief space, and sailed away.

My journey had another object. Cure had fared badly in the two balk-line tournaments in this country. His supporters said he was handicapped by being so far from home. So I wished to give him an opportunity to display his skill against me on his native soil.

# CHAPTER XXVIII

## I MAKE A WORLD'S RECORD RUN

PARIS seemed glad to see me back. The old Olympia Academy where I had played as a boy in short trousers ten years before, was crowded to the doors when I stepped to the table one afternoon late in February, 1912, to begin a series of exhibition matches against Cure.

In 1906 I had won the world's championship at 18.1 from the old idol of France, Maurice Vignaux. Now, the Frenchmen confidently hoped, Cure would make amends by trouncing me soundly at 18.2. But their hopes were not well founded. I never played better billiards in my life, than in that week of exhibition matches against the famous French professional.

Not only did I beat him soundly, 6 matches out of seven, but I made a new world's record high run.

I have often looked back to that afternoon at the Olympia and thought over all the conditions, the table, the crowd, my own mental attitude, that made it possible for me to make a world's record run without losing control of the balls. In the first place, during the earlier sessions, I had become thoroughly accustomed to the cloth. The balls were lively and true. The temperature of the academy was uniformly warm, and there were no distracting influences around the table. Your French billiard fan rarely talks out loud, and he is better behaved than the restless American.

It was exactly a quarter past 3 o'clock when I took my turn at the table. The balls were in the lower section, about eighteen inches apart, with my cue ball in the center.

With one or two drives and a draw, I had them together. The first two hundred points were made at the foot of the table in close position. Then they became unruly there, and after two or three wide angle shots, I transferred them to the head section, where I soon had them astride a balk line, nicely placed.

My stroke was never better, and the balls responded perfectly. For fifteen or twenty minutes at a time I would keep them within a radius of four or five inches, at the intersection of the balk lines, driving occasionally to the side rail as position required.

The referee's voice droned on, counting in French.

I finished my string of 500 points in less than an hour. The crowd clamored for me to go on. A few minutes later when I passed 531, beating the record run made by Cure a few days before my arrival, the spectators gave me such a hearty burst of applause that I had to stop and rest a minute until the tumult died down. Then, freshly sand-papering and chalking my cue, I kept on. At 600 there was another outburst of cheering. Soon after that the balls became unruly. Finally in an hour and twenty minutes I missed on a difficult follow shot.

I had run 622 billiards.

Not until the run was over and I was unscrewing my cue did I feel the slightest fatigue. Then, with the intense concentration lifted from my mind, I felt very tired.

That is the longest run I ever made. Frequently in exhibition matches, however, I have made un-finished strings of 300 and 400, and quit with the balls in good position.

While we are on the subject of record runs, I would like to recall a curious freak that occurred during an exhibition match with Charley Peterson at Los Angeles in 1915. I won the bank and made the opening shot, gathering the balls in the upper left hand corner at the intersection of the balk line. In that position I ran out my string of 250 points. At no time during the run were the object balls more than four inches apart. I did not have to resort to a single drive to the foot of the table, nor did any one of the balls touch the right hand rail. All the drives were made against the left hand side rail and the upper end rail.

Charley Peterson made a map of that run, which I have preserved in my scrap book. Together with my run of 622 points in Paris, it represents my highest achievement in balk line control.

The crowds that flocked to the Olympia during my matches with Cure and the interest displayed by the public about that time in billiards once again drew down the wrath of the French Government. Gambling on our games had reached a point where the officials felt called upon to take steps against it. Inasmuch as a high French court had ruled that billiards was a game of skill and not one of chance, the Government could not suppress the academies under their gambling laws. They did the next thing, issued an order banishing foreign billiard players.

Obviously, the order was directed against me. The academy management appealed the case, pointing out that they were obligated to pay me $3,000 for my series of exhibitions, but the Government was firm.

We obtained a stay of execution until March 17.

During that interval I met several other leading French players, including Cassignol and Adjoran, winning 38 out of a total of 45 matches played, **and averaging better than 40.**

# CHAPTER XXIX

## WHAT IT COSTS TO KEEP THE BILLIARD CROWN

THE billiard championship of the world is worth from $20,000 to $50,000 a year to the winner. But the champion pays a very definite price to keep his title. Just as a great singer must guard his voice against colds and over exertion, so a billiard champion must take ceaseless care of his arm.

In an earlier chapter I told how my father developed my game to championship form. Whether I could keep that form and remain long at the top depended solely on my own efforts. Having grown past the voting age I couldn't expect my father to stand continually at my elbow telling me what to do and what not to do, and threatening dire consequences if I failed. No, from the time I won my second balk line championship, it was up to me.

I was very fond of baseball. Back in Cornwall I used to play with our High School team every summer. But a billiard champion can't take chances with his hands. So I had to give it up. I could

143

toss a ball and play catch, occasionally, but no
batting or strenuous fielding.   I couldn't even run
the risk of getting heavy callouses on my palms.

Golf proved a pleasant diversion for a while.   I
bought a nice new set of sticks, learned how to swing
and follow through, and was getting to the point
where I played a pretty fair game.   Then suddenly
I noticed a kink in my forearm.   The golf muscles
were getting mixed up with the billiard muscles.
So golf, too, had to go.   I gave my sticks to my
kid brother, and looked around for something else.

Tennis was out of the question.   It was too great
a strain on my wrist.   So, by a process of elimina-
tion, walking and swimming were the only strenuous
outdoor activities I could engage in.

I had to be careful of my eyes, too.   They had
always been dependable, but I realized I couldn't
afford to abuse them.   In training for a championship match, I have gone for days without reading
the ordinary type in a newspaper.   The headlines
were all I would take a chance on.   Whenever I
found anything particularly interesting, I would
ask one of my sisters to read it to me.

And by the way, I would advise any young man
who seeks to make himself billiard champion to
provide himself with a couple of sisters.   Give
them a little elemental knowledge of the game and
they can tell you exactly how every shot should be

made. They make a good audience, too. My sisters sit in the family box with my mother every time I play a championship match, and after it is over they can tell me all about it every time, just why I tripped up on such and such a shot, and how I should have played it.

Another thing a billiard player has to watch is his bedtime. Sleep is the greatest thing in the world to restore nerve force, and unless a billiard player gets plenty of sleep, at regular hours, he might as well put aside his cue and take up bowling. I have always made it a practice to go to bed early and rise early in the morning. Then in the afternoon I take a nap between four and six.

I have never taken a drink of alcoholic liquor, nor smoked a cigar or cigarette. My father smoked and drank a good deal, yet at the same time he made it quite clear to me that those things weren't good for a growing young billiard player.

Now it is quite possible that I could smoke moderately and drink moderately and go on playing championship billiards. But there might come a time when my whole career hinged on a single shot, and the cue arm would falter just a fraction of an inch because of a little nicotine or alcohol somewhere in my nervous system. I can't afford to take any chances.

Hard work, more than anything else, keeps me in

trim. From the beginning of the billiard season, early in October until the following June I spend at least five hours a day walking around a billiard table, bending over, twisting, using both hands, bring all the muscles in my body and most of my nerves into action. I am healthily tired every night.

During preparation for any important championship match I practice about four hours a day until four days before the match. Then I "taper off" to an hour a day for two days. The day before the match I take a long walk, and don't go near a billiard table.

On the day of the match, I take lots of fresh air in the morning, take a walk again in the afternoon, eat a light dinner about two or two-thirty and then take a nap. At 5 o'clock I get up and dress and spend about fifteen minutes at a billiard table, warming up my stroke. Then I devote ten or fifteen minutes more to examining my cue tips and shafts, testing them to see that the leather is firm and well shaped, and sandpapering the shafts to make them slide easily through my hand. I always carry two extra shafts into every match, in case a tip should split or come off.

In these small essentials, as well as the major requisites of stroke and strategy, a billiard champion cannot afford to take any chances.

From November, 1911, to June, 1912, I played

four challenge matches in which my world's championship was at stake. I was keenly on my game, and won them all. I defeated Sutton at Madison Square Garden, November 11, 1911, 500 to 266; again in February, 1912, I defeated Sutton at the Hotel Astor 500 to 280. Calvin Demarest challenged and I defeated him at the Hotel Astor, April 11, 500 to 440. In June came Harry Cline's turn. Score (at Horticultural Hall, Philadelphia) Hoppe, 500; Cline, 396.

Having defended the championship trophy two years it now became my permanent property.

# CHAPTER XXX

## A MATCH WITH YAMADA—ORIENTAL TEMPERAMENT

KOJI YAMADA of Japan defeated me in one game of the fifth balk line tournament, held at the Hotel Astor Roof Garden in November, 1912. With three points to go, I missed a difficult massé shot and he came from behind to win, 500 to 497. That was the only defeat I sustained in the tournament, and I held my championship. The other players, all of whom I defeated were Slosson, Morningstar, Cline, Demarest, Sutton and Al Taylor.

Yamada finished third, and immediately after the tournament was ended a great clamor arose for a match between us. If the Japanese could beat me once, why couldn't he do it again?

After disposing of George Sutton in a challenge match at the Hotel Astor in February (500 to 301) I went on tour for several months, meanwhile preparing for the inevitable challenge match with Yamada. It finally came off in May of that year. The Hotel Astor again was the scene.

The Grand Ball Room was crowded with spectators, many of whom were Yamada's countrymen. They sat there large-eyed and expectant, tense with the hope that their champion might win the world's title for the glory of old Japan.

Perhaps this was too big a mental hazard for Yamada to overcome. At any rate, he played uncertainly and the ivory balls refused to do his bidding. As for myself, I was determined not only to keep the championship safe in the United States but to wipe out that tournament defeat, which still rankled.

I played at the top of my game, running out the string of 500 points in twelve innings for an average of 41.66. Meanwhile Yamada had collected only 33 caroms for an average of 3.

Later I made an exhibition tour with Yamada as a playing partner, and found him to be an excellent billiard player, with a massé stroke that compared with the greatest experts, not excepting Schaefer or Horemans. He had learned most of his billiards in Berlin, while attending a university there. Following his rise to the front rank of professionals, billiards experienced a big boom in Japan, and the younger crop of players, Tadao Suganuma, Kinrey Matsuyama and K. Odati, all developed under his tutelage.

In passing, let me say a word about the Japanese billiard temperament. They are agile, dexterous, quick to learn. A number of writers on billiards have pointed out that the Japanese temperament is ideally suited to the game because they are stoical, calm, impassive, no matter how badly the balls break. This is a superficial view.

The Japanese player maintains a calm exterior in the face of adversity. His face never betrays emotion. But all the while he is burning up inside. I have watched them time after time, sitting in the chair after an unfortunate miss, and noticed a peculiar expression deep in the eyes and a convulsive movement of the muscles of the jaw, that betrayed their real state of mind.

Your American player is generally frank and emphatic in his disgust. Sometimes he gives vent to an explosive "damn!" when the balls roll awry, or he misses a shot through carelessness. Not a few of them talk sternly to themselves as they return to their chair. That, to my mind, is the healthier way to work off your emotion. It doesn't pay to burn up inside.

My victory over Yamada marked the end of a definite period in my career. Thereafter for a period of six years and a half I was to hold the 18.2 championship without challenge. This was partly due to the war, which made competitive billiards impossible, and partly to the fact that no balk line player emerged of a caliber to test my supremacy.

Let me sum up this early period in brief review. Since I won my first world's championship from Maurice Vignaux in Paris, February 15, 1906, I had taken part in 25 championship matches. Of these, 13 were in tournament play; twelve were challenge matches.

The summarized results were as follows:

Challenge matches won, 11; lost 1 : tournament matches won, 9; lost 4. Total points, Hoppe, 10,606; opponents, 7,763.

# CHAPTER XXXI

## I WIN FROM MELBOURNE INMAN, THE ENGLISH PLAYER

WHEN the war broke out in the summer of 1914, Melbourne Inman, champion of the world at English billiards left England, where all sports were abruptly terminated, and came to the United States. His manager, R. L. Benjamin, issued a sweeping challenge to me for the world's championship of the green cloth, to be decided in a series of matches at both English and American styles of the game.

He suggested a long contest, with series of matches in New York City, Chicago, Montreal, Winnepeg and Toronto, six days of play in each city.

The proposition sounded attractive and I accepted. For two weeks I practiced steadily at the English game on one of their huge tables, 6 feet wide by 12 feet long, the balls slightly smaller than the regulation 3.3-8 inch championship size. I found I had to learn the game all over again. The whole theory of scoring and position play was different.

SETTLING DOWN TO A LONG LEFT-HANDED DRAW

The champion plays almost equally well with both hands, rarely resorting to the bridge.

The English game is played on a table with six pockets. An ordinary carom counts 2, pocketing the red ball counts 3, making a 'hazard' (i.e. sending your cue ball in the pocket) off the red, 3; a hazard off your opponent's ball, 2; pocketing your opponent's ball 2. Thus, they have a variety of alternatives on each shot, and the game is greatly diversified.

I could hold my own at caroms, despite the difficulty of handling smaller balls, and I was fairly accurate at pocketing the red, but when it came to hazards I was all at sea. Those pockets were so small and so contrary. Time after time I would send my cue ball skimming for the corner, only to see it catch in the jaw and hang there, refusing to go down.

I used to marvel at Inman's accuracy on these shots. With a long graceful sweep of his cue he would send his ball shooting off the red in mid-table, to plop straight as a die in the corner pocket. From any angle, with that same sweeping stroke, he could score hazards at will. I used to wonder, too, at the way he held his cue. Catching it in the tips of his fingers, he seemed to play with a stiff wrist, most of the work being done with the forearm.

By diligent practice I gained a fair technique at the English game and when we played the first

match at the Hotel Astor ball room the night of
September 29, 1914, I succeeded in rolling up 304
while Inman was completing his string of 600.
That night they took the table down and substituted
a regulation 5 x 10 American balk line table for the
following day's matches at my style of game.

The balk line matches were even more one-sided.
I scored 1,000 points in two sessions against Inman's total of 295. His stroke was too solid for
the American game. He made some difficult shots
in open table, but when it came to close position
play, he was lost. He didn't have the touch nor
the delicacy of stroke to hold them on the line,
where we in America make the most of our points.

The following day, in two sessions of English
billiards I scored 621 points while Inman was ac-
cumulating 1,200. At the end of the week it was
clearly demonstrated that I could outplay him 5
to 1 at balk line, whereas he could play me only 2
to 1 at his own game. We went on to Chicago,
played our week's engagement there and thence to
Montreal; but by this time the score was so lop-
sided in my favor that the so-called "World's Championship" became a farce.

I noticed one peculiarity of Inman's play, which
I have since learned is characteristic of all English
players. He could massé fairly well from left to
right, but when it came to a back-hand massé, he

was lost. He couldn't make a bridge for a back-hand massé. Consequently his nursing suffered by the absence of this valuable stroke.

In addition to winning another "championship" at this hybrid game, I also acquired a manager. Mr. Benjamin made a deal at the end of our tour whereby he took charge of my business affairs, booking engagements, taking care of the press notices, handling the sale of tickets, and fulfilling all the functions my father toiled at when we were barnstorming about the country years before.

Mr. Benjamin performed his duties with a flourish. It was he who, co-operating with the Red Cross and other war time agencies, arranged a series of billiard benefits which raised, through the medium of my cue, more than $50,000 for relief work, ambulances, etc.

All competition was suspended of course, through the years from 1914 to 1919. Not a single challenge match was held, nor a tournament played during that interval, so thoroughly was billiards mobilized for war purposes.

In the meantime two young billiard players were developing out west. Reports began to reach New York of the remarkable performances by a boy named Young Jake Schaefer, and of another youngster, Welker Cochran.

They had frequently been reported to have made

runs of 100 and better at 18.2.   Along toward
1919, when the war clouds began to clear away,
they began an invasion of the East.   They were
looking for me, and their intentions were plain.
They wanted the billiard crown I had been wearing
so long.

# CHAPTER XXXII

### THE YOUNGER GENERATION—SCHAEFER AND COCHRAN—ANOTHER TILT FOR MY TITLE

YOUNG JAKE SCHAEFER was not altogether a stranger to me when he came East, in 1919, to compete in a balk line tournament at the Hotel Astor for the world's championship. I remember him first as a lad of about 3 or 4, who used to toddle around the Schaefer home in Paris, when I was playing my first engagement at the Olympia Academy there, in 1901. At that time he was too young to hold a cue, much less poke it at the balls with any idea of the consequences.

But, as the son of an illustrious father, it was only natural that he should get into the game as soon as he grew tall enough to stand at the table. I have a picture of him practicing under the watchful eye of his father at the age of 10 or thereabouts.

Young Jake came by his billiards naturally, if ever a youngster did. But there was this difference between his early career and mine. His father was too busy playing billiards, travelling about the country, and earning the family livelihood with his cue to give a great deal of attention to the boy's early billiard education. The family income did not depend, as in my own case, upon the skill of the "Boy Wonder." So the youngster picked up the game piecemeal from his father, without the benefit of those long hours of toil and tribulation that pounded the game into my head at an early age.

Following his father's death Young Jake while still in short trousers had made a tour with Ora Morningstar. At that time—about 1908 or 1909—he could already average 10 or 12 at balk line. His stroke was very similar to mine with the right forearm held out at the side of the head and the wrist doing its work with a lateral motion instead of the pendulum swing.

Billiard writers call this style "unorthodox." Yet it has produced the only two world's champions in the last fifteen years.

I came in closer contact with Schaefer during a long tour to the Pacific Coast in 1916. There was quite a troupe of billiard players in our party which included beside Schaefer and myself, Chick Wright of San Francisco and Charley Peterson of St. Louis, the famous fancy shot player.

Schaefer was already showing the ear marks of a fine player. Frequently during the exhibition work on that tour he made runs of 100 and better and on several occasions defeated me in 300 point matches.

Cochran, I did not know so well. He had received most of his billiard training under Morningstar in Chicago, and under the veteran teacher, Perkins.

The sixth balk line tournament at 18.2, held at the Hotel Astor Grand Ball Room in October, 1912, saw both Schaefer and Cochran among the entrants. In addition were a number of old familiar faces. Sutton, Slosson and Morningstar were on hand again, and Yamada, who held a victory over me in the 1912 tournament, was eager for another chance.

After a lapse of six years and a half, during which interval many things might happen to a billiard champion's arm and his nerve, the followers of the game were wondering if the time had come to crown a new champion. There was a good deal of sentimental interest in Sutton and Slosson, those hardy perennials of billiard competition. Morningstar's experience was counted heavily in his favor, and the two youngsters Cochran and Schaefer were conceded to be a likely pair of dark horses, even if they were only yearlings.

The long lay-off apparently had done me good. I was unbeatable and unbeaten, romping through the tournament with six straight victories, a grand average of 45.28 and a single average (against Sutton) of 80. Morningstar finished second, with a grand average of 26.06, nearly twenty points below me.

The two youngsters, Schaefer and Cochran, finished third and fourth, and between them, they divided other honors, too. Cochran made the high run of the tournament, and the highest ever recorded up to that time in a championship event, 265, in his game against Slosson. Schaefer averaged 80 against Yamada, beating him 400 to 82.

They had shown flashes of real championship form, sufficient to justify the prediction that before long they would threaten my long-held supremacy.

Old timers who sat through the matches at the Astor said that Young Jake's game was only vaguely reminiscent of his famous father's. The Wizard was short of stature and dark, while Young Schaefer was tall, slender and fair-haired. Long legs and a long reach enabled him to make almost any shot on the table without resorting to a bridge. Maurice Daly said he had the most perfect "dead ball" since Frank Ives.

Although he had perfect technique and form at the table, Young Jake was an erratic performer that year. Good one day, terrible the next.

Cochran, too, was an in and outer, playing superbly against Morningstar and Slosson; falling down badly against Yamada and me. Students of billiard form, however, remarked upon his easy graceful stroke, his firm bridge hand, and his good judgment of second ball play.

From my own observation of Cochran's play, I have this criticism to make. He plays his draw shots with too much spin, knocking the second object ball further away than is necessary. If he would tone his draw down a bit and practice more regularly, he would be one of the hardest players in the world to beat.

These new faces lent a livelier interest to post-war billiard competition. The following year the tournament was limited to a three-man affair, Schaefer, Cochran and myself. We played twice around, and while I did not lose a game, Schaefer and Cochran broke even. I had a narrow escape in my first match with Cochran. He had me 370 to 366, and then missed with only 30 more to go. I won the rest of my matches easily, and so emerged from another tournament with the championship safely in my possession.

# CHAPTER XXXIII

### THE FOREIGN INVASION

In the winter of 1920-21 came a lull in billiard competition. It was a calm before the storm.

Schaefer and Cochran had failed to win a single game from me in the 3-man tournament held at the Hotel Astor in December. In the four matches I had scored 1,600 points to their combined total of 740. The old-timers Sutton and Slosson had dropped temporarily out of the picture.

A querulous note crept into the newspaper sporting pages: "why doesn't somebody come along and beat this fellow Hoppe?" Even the billiard fans took to yawning a little bit as I continued my string of victories, unbroken since 1911.

Things had reached this desultory stage when a steamer from Antwerp deposited one day a stocky, dark haired person on the New York waterfront. Under his arm he carried a long bundle, which, when unwrapped, revealed a number of billiard cues. His name was Edouard Horemans.

What was his purpose in migrating to these shores?  To play the billiards.  Would he kindly step forward and do his stuff?  He would—and did!

Horemans was a sensation.  Left-handed, slow and heavy of foot, he moved about the table with a ponderous grace, wagging his head from side to side with the air of a fatalist at each successive maneuver of the balls.

A little handful of spectators who saw him play his first exhibition match at Daly's sat spellbound. Here was a new stroke, and a new strategy.  The Belgian's stroke was little more than a jab, a solid substantial poke at the balls, with very few preliminaries.  He wasted neither time nor muscle at preliminary cueing.  Withal he got amazing accuracy and timing in his close range manipulation.  So much for his stroke.

His strategy was even more astonishing.  The billiard fans were amazed to see him shun the end table, and march the balls out into the center panel at the first opportunity.  There in the unrestricted space, with the two side rails as his only boundaries, he scored most of his caroms.

But the most amazing thing of all was his massé. Time after time the Belgian would put his cue up in the air, bring it down deftly and surely on top of his ball and execute that sharp curve which is so fraught with possibilities and hedged about with danger.

Almost as soon as he had gotten rid of his sea legs, Horemans began to make phenomenal runs. Several times he passed the 500 mark, and on one occasion, at the Amateur Billiard Club he made a run of 800.   And always he used the same scoring method, center panel nurse, that short jab draw, and the massé, which he executed at all angles and in the most difficult positions.

Horemans' boyhood, it seemed, had been spent in a parochial school in Belgium.   Among the recreations of the priests was a billiard table.   Beginning at the age of 16, he had practised faithfully at this table until, within the short space of a few years he had made himself champion of Europe.

Someone asked him how he had ever perfected such a marvellous massé shot.

"Six hours practice a day for four years," he replied.

As soon as his marvelous talents became known, there was a great clamor for a challenge match for my championship.   But first Horemans engaged in a match with Young Jake Schaefer at Daly's Academy.   Playing exceptionally fine billiards he forged ahead of the young American, and led him by nearly 500 points on the last day of the match. Then Young Jake steadied down, played the mar-

velous game he is capable of, ran 426 and caught
Horemans in the last night's play to win by a scant
margin.

That match acted as a brisk stimulant to billiard
interest in this country.   It revealed Horemans' as
a capable performer, but more especially it revealed
Young Jake's fighting qualities and his steadiness
under fire.

There was a reason for Young Jake's comeback.
at Graney's Academy in San Francisco.   Red ball
is a far different game from balk line, and it gives
no opportunity for close nursing practice.   In the
winter of 1920, Graney's had closed, and Young
Jake, instead of returning to the Pacific Coast, had
devoted himself to serious balk line practice.

After his match with Horemans, he loomed up
more than ever, as a dangerous contender for my
title.

In spite of Horeman's defeat, there was still talk
of a match with me that Spring.   His manager made
a great deal of conversation about a long match at
18.1, preferably 3,000 or 4,000 points for the
world's championship; and my manager made still
more conversation about the size of the side bet.
Charges of unsportsmanship, cowardice and "dog
in the manger" were passed around briskly.   Sparks
began to fly.

Altogether, the situation reminded old timers of the days when Frank Ives and Jacob Schaefer the Elder used to write long letters to the newspapers. In short, interest was picking up.

About this time another foreigner invaded our shores. He, too, had come to play the billiards. His name was Roger Conti, and his title, Champion of France.

Spring and summer passed with a great clatter of cues, and whirring sound of ivory balls. Everybody was looking forward to autumn, when a great billiard tournament would bring Horemans, Conti, Schaefer and myself with a number of other players, together in Chicago. And well they might look forward to it, for that tournament was destined to make balk line history. An old champion was to be overthrown and a new one crowned!

# CHAPTER XXXIV

## AN OLD CHAMPION OVERTHROWN, AND A NEW ONE CROWNED

I HAVE played in fifteen or twenty billiard tournaments in my long career, but none could compare with the eighth balk line championship held in Chicago in November, 1921. Like the Dempsey-Firpo fight, it was in a class by itself.

Consider the dramatic setting. Horemans and Conti, sensational dark horses from Europe had come 4,000 miles to contest for the championship. Young Jake Schaefer was playing in his old home town. Two veterans, George Butler Sutton and Ora Morningstar had chalked their cues for a comeback. Cochran was a likely contender.

As for myself, the drama was not lacking. Here was the stiffest opposition I had met in 15 years. A new school, a younger and more daring generation was forging to the front. Could I withstand them?

And back of it all, dangled the world's championship, a title that meant $25,000 or $30,000 during the next year to the winner.

Young Jake had the bit between his teeth. He romped through the early matches, bowling over Morningstar, Sutton, and Horemans as if they had been nine pins. He lost one game—played in the afternoon—to Roger Conti, but he more than made amends for it a night or two later when he defeated Cochran 400 to nothing, running 82 points from the spot, and then, after Cochran had had one shot and missed, running the game out with a finely played 318. That average of 200 broke all records for tournament play and is likely to stand for some years to come.

One of the dramatic climaxes of the tournament was my match with Horemans. After all the talk that had passed between our managers, there was a tense rivalry manifest as we stepped to the table in the fifteenth game of the tournament.

Horemans was nervous and not at all sure of himself. On the other hand, I was off my game. We played mediocre billiards all the way through. With victory in sight, Horemans tripped up when he needed only 21, and I ran the game out. A comparison of averages showed that he had made 21.055 to my 21.052, another one of those freaks of billiards where the loser, denied the opening shot, makes a higher average than the winner.

We came down to the last night of the tournament. Schaefer had won four games and lost one. I had won five in a row. If I could win over Schaefer, the championship was mine again. If he defeated me, we were tied for first place.

You could have heard a pin drop in the Auditorium Annex that night when the referee called Schaefer and me to the table. Every seat was filled and in the galleries upstairs, the "dollar-a-throw" boys were banked so deep that those in the rear could only wonder what was going on from the outbursts of applause.

The applause was all for Jake. I spent the evening holding my cue, watching the championship slip away from me as Jake worked skillfully at the table, piling up an unbeatable total of points.

What does a billiard player think about as he sits in his chair, brooding over lost opportunities? His mind is a curious vacuum. Past errors rise up to reproach him. He wonders what the total "gate" amounts to as his eye wanders all around the crowded seats. Will that fellow at the table never miss? And all the while, out of the corner of his eye, he is watching the shifting balls, and listening for the false click that will tell him his opponent has missed.

Jake's misses were few and far between that night. He ran out his string in 6 innings for an average of 66.66, while I was laboriously collecting 26 caroms for an average of 4.23. Writing about the match later, in his "History of the 18.2 Balk Line Game," Thomas J. Gallegher said:

"That performance may be termed a freak, for it was not in any respect an exposition of Hoppe's skill or courage. He simply could not get control of the ivories and in six innings made meager scores of 15, 7, 4 and three ciphers."

Now we were tied for the championship. The play-off came the night of December 22. Schaefer won again, but not without a struggle. He ran 500 points in 6 innings for the remarkable average of 83.33, while I was collecting 346 in 5 innings for an average of 69.2. I did my best but it was not quite enough.

I shall never forget my sombre reflections during the latter part of the game as I sat in my chair, watching Schaefer, like a finely tuned mechanism, click off the points. Was this the end of my career?

Is that tall youngster, standing there at the table, bending so confidently over the balls destined to send me into the discard? Has he got something up his sleeve that I have lost—or never possessed?

Well, at any rate, my reign was over. The Boy Wonder of Cornwall Landing was now a has-been, with a sprinkling of grey hairs at the age of thirty-four, and an uncomfortable hitch in his arm.

Could I come back?

# CHAPTER XXXV

## THE COMEBACK

I HAD developed a serious hitch in my cue arm. Sometimes I would get set for a shot, fiddle back and forth with my cue a dozen times, and then find I couldn't let go.

A doctor gave me a thorough examination. With the exception of some bad teeth, I was in fairly good shape. A nerve specialist told me:

"It's a case of nervous exhaustion. That arm of yours is worn out. Give it rest. The wear and tear of thirty years was bound to tell on you sooner or later. There's nothing radically wrong. There is no disease that nature can't cure."

That was encouraging. In the challenge match against Young Jake Schaefer in Chicago March 27, 28 and 29, I had occasion again to test my cue arm, and try for my old championship. We were on even terms practically all through the match. On the last night, with Schaefer needing only ten points to win, I was making a desperate effort to run my

string out. I had only forty or thereabouts to go.
Suddenly the balls lined up near the side rail. A
massé was the only solution. I raised my cue and
carefully took aim.

For the space of a minute, I fiddled, trying to
release the co-ordinated control of eye and arm. But
I couldn't do it. My arm refused to obey. The
situation was tense. A fan way up in the topmost
balcony yelled:

"Go ahead, shoot!"

That seemed to relieve the tension. Everybody
laughed, and when things had settled down a bit, I
took aim again, shot, and made it.

Now a curious thing happened. I took careful
aim for a draw shot, went through the usual preliminaries,—and made a fatal miscue! From a favorable leave, Schaefer got the balls in hand and quickly
ran out the game.

Now this incident is not related as an alibi, to
blame the loss of the match on the overwrought fan
in the gallery. It wasn't his fault at all, because
I made the massé shot. But I think my arm was
so tired and strained from the long upright position,
that it failed to put enough punch in the draw stroke.
Or perhaps, it was just one of the breaks of the
game.

I lost the match, 1,500 to 1,468, but in losing it I
gained back a lot of my old time confidence.

Schaefer wasn't a superman, and I wasn't a has-been.

That summer I took a long rest. I didn't go near a billiard table for weeks at a time. I used my right arm for dressing and eating, and little else.

In the fall I slowly worked myself into condition again for tournament play. In pleasant weather I used to take a run in Central Park before breakfast every morning; then a long walk in the forenoon, with an hour or so at the billiard table just before lunch. I had a masseur work on my shoulder and my right arm twice a day for three months, putting new life in the old muscles, and sloughing off the old tissue.

When tournament time came around again, I was fit and ready.

There is this difference between a veteran billiard player and a youngster. The veteran knows all the tricks and resources of the table. He knows the pitfalls of being frozen on the cushion, the dangers that lurk in lineups. Every shot has a dozen warning signs posted around it for him, telling him what to do and what not to do.

The youngster, on the other hand, is supremely conscious of his own genius. He is confident that he can rise to any emergency. He plays surely, deftly and courageously. But when the breaks come, the veteran has all his background of experience to get him out of a hole, while the youngster finds his genius, sometimes, lacking in adversity.

So it was, that with my right arm rested and restored, I went into the Ninth Balk Line tournament, held in New York City at the Hotel Pennsylvania in November, 1922, prepared again to match my old time resourcefulness against the inspirational play of the youngsters.

My first game was against Horemans. If I had had any misgivings before, they were all dispelled when I defeated the Belgian 500 to 177, averaging 55.55 to his 16.99. Again, in the second game against Cochran I averaged 55.55 and turned him back 500 to 172.

Hagenlacher, the German entrant, gave me a stern battle. In this game, the old time hitch returned for a while, and on several shots I had to stop and rest before I could finally persuade my arm to launch the cue.

Schaefer, meanwhile, had lost a game to Horemans, and when we came together in the final match of the tournament, he had to beat me to tie for the championship, while all I needed was that one game to win back my old crown.

I won it. Sometimes they do come back.

# CHAPTER XXXVI

### HOW LONG CAN I KEEP MY TITLE?

A CERTAIN quiet old chap has been attending all my championship matches regularly for the last four or five years. He used to sit away up in the gallery and I didn't pay much attention to him. But recently he has been edging down to the front rows and once or twice he even climbed over the brass rail that surrounds the table and stood beside me as I chalked my cue.

Persistent old codger! His name is Father Time.

Whenever I miss he comes and stands beside my chair.

"Willie," he'll say: "you're getting on in years. That old arm isn't what it used to be. 'Bout time to put that cue of yours up in the rack."

Well . . . perhaps so. I've been champion through seventeen of the last eighteen years, and I guess I can't hold my titles forever. But let us take an inventory and see just where we stand.

As this is written (October, 1924) I have just passed my thirty-seventh birthday. That isn't so old. True enough, some prize fighters are through in their thirties, and baseball players rarely see forty in the big leagues. But boxing and baseball burn up a great deal of irreplaceable physical energy, and in both of those sports supremacy depends on speed.

Speed doesn't figure in the game of billiards. In this game it is nerve co-ordination that counts; that and a keen eye.

I expect to be playing as good a game of billiards at fifty as I am to-day at 37. That doesn't mean I'll be champion for thirteen years more. Some young phenomenon may bob up in the next year or two and knock me off the Christmas tree. Or Jacob Schaefer the Younger may find the balls rolling nicely in the next tournament and repeat his victories at Chicago.

But the point is this: I've taken mighty good care of myself. There isn't a drop of alcohol or nicotine in my system. In spite of long sieges of travel on the road, late hours and Pullman berths, I have had my share of sleep and rest.

As the years go on I find I have to watch my nerves and take better care of my right arm. But there isn't any reason why I can't continue to average from forty to sixty for the next twenty years. Schaefer played good billiards up to his late forties

## THE PRICE OF BILLIARD SUPREMACY

Clean living, plenty of outdoor exercise, and regular habits have been essential
factors in Willie Hoppe's long championship reign.

and Vignaux was champion at both 18.1 and 18.2 in his sixties, more than thirty years after he won his first world's championship in 1875.

As for the game of billiards itself, it is such a stimulating and fascinating study, that even if I were laid on the shelf as a champion, I should continue to play it as a pastime. And that reminds me of an incident that happened to me in Boston some years ago.

At the beginning of an exhibition match I noticed a man come in through the green curtains surrounding the exhibition space, stumble against a chair, and make his way haltingly to a seat near the table. A little later there was a commotion, he had taken another man's chair, and was forced to move back several rows.

Something about the man's hesitating walk, and a fixed expression on his face caused me to regard him closely. He was blind.

After the exhibition, as the crowd was leaving I went over and sat down beside him.

"Tell me," I said, "what enjoyment do you get out of a billiard exhibition when you can't see what's going on."

"It's true I can't see," he told me, "but I can hear. Sitting close to the table, I can tell by the click the kind of stuff you put on the ball. I used to be a pretty fair player before my sight failed, and you'd be surprised how much I can pick up just by listening.

"For instance, on a three cushion shot, the length of time between clicks tells me the cue ball has gone around the table. When you're nursing them, and making short dead ball drives, I can follow it very well. Then, too, the referee's counting, and his 'in' and 'out' all help me to follow the game."

Blind! And yet in this game of twirling ivory balls he found escape and diversion.

There is a man in a wheel chair who comes to my billiard academy in New York every Saturday about 11 o'clock and plays all through the afternoon. He pulls himself about the table, rolling the chair into position and handling his cue with surprising dexterity. He uses the bridge a good deal. Massé shots, of course, are out of the question, but otherwise he plays a good sound game.

He tells me that billiards is practically the only exercise he gets.

"But I don't play it for the exercise," he once said; "I play it for the fun I get out of it."

Barred forever from all other sports, he finds recreation and diversion in billiards. It is the greatest game in the world.

A banker in Nashville, Tenn., once told me a story.

"We had a young auditor here at the bank," he

said, "who used to go out to lunch about twelve o'clock and stay until two. Where he went nobody knew. One day we were discussing him at a directors' meeting and the president sent for him.

" 'Tell us, Jones,' said the president, 'what do you do with your time every day between twelve o'clock and two?' The young fellow stammered and was obviously flustered.

" 'Well,' he said 'it's this way. I come down here in the morning at 8:30 and work over the books for three hours and a half. When noon comes my head is all cluttered up with figures. Sixes and sevens and naughts are all whirling around before my eyes, and I'm pretty well fagged out wrestling with them.

" 'I go over to the hotel billiard room and get a sandwich and a glass of milk and for two hours I play billiards. I don't bet on the games. I only play for the fun of the thing, and to get all those figures out of my head.

" 'When I get back to the bank in the afternoon I feel able to tackle the books again. I'm sorry that I've been staying out to lunch so long. I'll try to get back earlier.'

" 'That's all right,' said the president, 'I didn't call you in here to call you down. Your work has been very good, particularly in the afternoons. We were just wondering how you spent your lunch hour, and wishing the rest of our bookkeepers would do the same.' "

It is a game that gives back, in healthy, stimulating recreation, twofold for all you put in it.

Billiards has done a great deal for me. Its green cloth has been a magic carpet, lifting me from obscurity in a small town, whisking me away to great cities and foreign lands, affording me an opportunity to travel and observe.

In addition to its ample rewards in money and adventure, the game has provided a stimulating mental pursuit. There is a fascination about the subjection of three ivory balls, in the study of their whims and caprices, their moods and fancies.

But before you can conquer the three rebellious ivory balls and make them do your bidding, you must first conquer yourself. And so I have found billiards to be more than a game; I have found it a philosophy of self-control.

In setting down this narrative of my life and my billiard career I am discharging an obligation that has grown increasingly heavy with the passing years. It is only fair that I should endeavor, in my limited way, to do something constructive and lasting for the game that has done so much for me.

If in this narrative and the lessons that accompany it I can encourage, arouse the imagination and stimulate the endeavors of even a few hundred of the great, loyal army of billiard players; if I can help them play their "dead ball" with a little more firmness and decision, and finally, if I can impart in some measure my billiard philosophy of self-control, I shall consider myself amply repaid.

# LESSON NO. 1

Mastery of the game of billiards is largely a state of mind. The mental attitude can be summed up simply in these three things:

1—Knowing what you can do;
2—Knowing what you want to do;
3—Concentrating on the immediate shot.

Charley Peterson's famous billiard battle-cry "Show me a shot I can't make" is a good psychological starting point. Charley has demonstrated that it is possible to make any shot on the billiard table. Nobody has yet been able to place the balls in such a difficult position that Charley couldn't connect for a carom. And if Charley Peterson can do it, so can you. That's the first point. Get it firmly fixed in your mind. You *can* make any shot on the table.

Knowing what you *want* to do is a little more complicated. You want to count—that's certain—and make the next shot easy. Position play is the thing. Plan. Scheme. Use your imagination. Try to picture where all three balls will be when they stop rolling on the next shot.

And now for the third point—Concentrate! Keep your mind focussed on that little diagram of ivory that lies before you. Harness your brain and don't let it wander off and begin to jump fences just as you are about to shoot. Keep your faculties keenly alert on the immediate problem and don't relax until your cue tip has gone through and finished its job. Concentrate! It's the greatest mental exercise in the world, in billiards or anything else.

*No. 1.—Keep your eye on the ball—and concentrate!*

# LESSON NO. 2

## THE STROKE.   (Center Ball.)

Take a single billiard ball and place it on the spot at the head of the table.   Aiming at the middle of the lower rail, strike your cue ball easily, in the center, and see how nearly you can make it return to the exact spot where you struck it.   Notice whether you have a tendency to give it a slight twist to one side or the other.

Practice going through the ball with the tip of your cue with an easy, crisp stroke, until your cue tip touches the cloth four inches beyond the original point of contact.   Watch how the drag you impart to the ball holds it steadily to the line.

Now strike your ball slightly above center with the same smooth stroke and try again to make it return accurately from the lower rail.   Try both shots at varying speeds and watch the effect off the cushion.

The course of the cue ball depends not only on where you hit it, but how your cue-tip follows through.   If you can shoot a straight ball, without a hair-line of deviation to left or right, and with a finished stroke, draw, follow and center ball, you are well equipped to start the game right.

Practise this stroke, half an hour at a time, for three or four days.   You have nothing else on the table to distract you.   You are not trying to make your cue ball perform any miracles, or follow any complicated course.   You are not disturbed by the presence of other balls.   You have a single objective —stick to it until the end is attained—a clean-cut, accurate center ball stroke in which you can repose confidence.

No. 2.—*Practice a center ball stroke without twist or " English."*

# LESSON NO. 3

The magic of the billiard stroke lies in the wrist. Your fore-arm swinging like a pendulum from the elbow, launches the cue forward to the point of contact with the ball. It acts as a piston, supplying the major power. Then the wrist, at the moment of contact, snaps the cue-tip through the ivory, refining the power of the arm to an even smoothness, stepping it up to the last notch of speed and follow-through, as the stroke requires.

The wrist is an universal joint, capable of twisting the ball during that last split second of the stroke to the right or left in an infinite variety of angles.

In making a draw shot the wrist at the moment of impact lifts the butt of the cue, sending the tip briskly forward and downward through the ball, and imparting the necessary back-spin.

To realize the importance of a flexible wrist, try making a draw shot, or any other shot requiring twist with the wrist held rigid as if it were a solid continuation of the forearm. Then, after you have witnessed the sorry result, try the same shot with the wrist performing its proper function.

Flexibility does not mean looseness. In your attempt to get a lively wrist action, do not relax your grip of the cue. Hold it lightly but firmly between the thumb and the palm. Sometimes it helps to tighten the grip a trifle just as the cue-tip strikes the ball, but do not make a practice of it if it results in a cramped wrist action.

The wrist puts the velvet touch in your billiard **stroke. Give it free play and watch the result.**

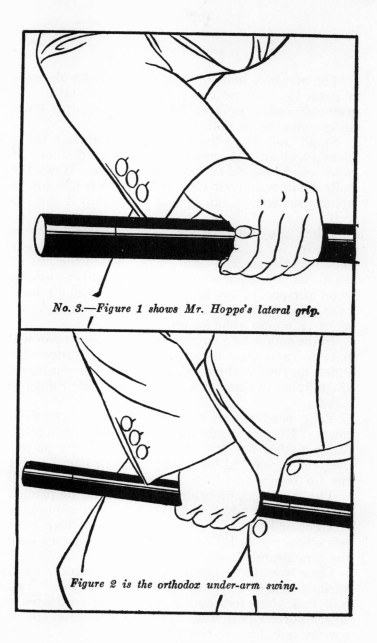

No. 3.—*Figure 1 shows Mr. Hoppe's lateral grip.*

*Figure 2 is the orthodox under-arm swing.*

# LESSON NO. 4

## THE STANCE

The accuracy and timing of your stroke depends a great deal on how you stand at the table. A well-balanced, firm-footed stance in billiards is quite as essential as in golf or baseball.

Stand well up to the table, with your feet fairly close together. If you are right-handed, most of your weight should be on the right foot. When the balls are in close formation and easy to reach, forget about your feet. Lean against the table if it steadies you.

When the balls are spread, and careful aim is necessary for a long shot, plant your feet firmly—as shown in the sketch—and get down into the line of play. Crouch over your cue until your eyes have a good perspective on the situation; but don't bend over so far you are in danger of losing your balance, or of cramping your swing.

In the course of a single game of billiards you will have to twist your body in a score of strange attitudes, no two of them exactly alike. Obviously, no single rule can apply to all. But keep these things in mind:

Your head is the range-finder and observation tower. Keep it steady until the stroke is complete. Many a shot has been missed because the player, over-eager, wagged his head just as he launched his cue tip forward.

The left hand, or bridge hand, should be planted firmly on the table, and the left arm should be straight and rigid. It is a good idea to turn your left elbow up as far as it will go, in order to keep the arm straight and firm.

Once you have acquired a good stance, these various details will take care of themselves. You will find your feet and arms moving instinctively to the correct positions. The thing to strive for is correct technique at the start.

*No. 4.—"Settling down" to a long, difficult shot. Note the firmness of stance, and the crouch which brings the eyes down in the line of play.*

# LESSON NO. 5

## THE DRAW

Old Michael Phelan used to teach beginners to make draw shots by placing two balls about six inches apart and then making a chalk mark on the cloth half way between. The pupil was told to aim low and drive his cue clear through to the chalk mark regardless of the ball.

That is sound advice. But let us consider the stroke a little further. The draw is the most valuable, by 33⅓ per cent, of all the strokes in billiards. Therefore it is worthy of a major portion of study and practice.

When you send your cue through the ball, do not be in a hurry to pull it back. Let the ball have that last, finishing caress, for it is by far the most important part of the stroke. As your cue-tip nears the table bed, still clinging to the ivory surface, it is working on the circumference at an effective angle. Give it a chance to finish the job!

Novices often think they can make the draw action more forceful by elevating the butt of the cue as they deliver the stroke. That is wrong. When you raise your cue handle, you restrict the follow-through, for the cue-tip goes too quickly to the cloth. *Keep your cue handle low!*

Another thing: do not let your cue-tip waver or wobble at the last moment of the stroke. The slightest indecision, the slightest variation from the line will be magnified as the ball comes back to its objective, and probably result in a miss. To aim right is not enough. Keep your mind and your cue-tip focussed on the pin-point you want to strike, and hold them both there until the stroke is complete.

Unless you have to remove your cue hurriedly to get out of the way of the returning ball, keep it in the finished position for a second or two. That will help the style and "finish" of your game.

Concentrate—follow through with the wrist—and hold it!

That's the secret of the draw.

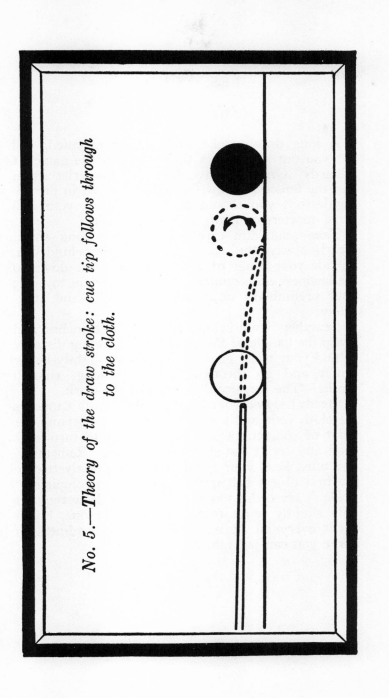

*No. 5.—Theory of the draw stroke: cue tip follows through to the cloth.*

# LESSON NO. 6

## THE LONG DRAW

A long draw stroke, successfully executed, will get you out of many a tight place in the game of billiards. Once you have developed the wrist action and the finished follow-through described in preceding lessons you should be able to draw your ball three quarters of the length of the table.

Take your aim carefully on these long shots. Nearly always the second object ball is behind you, outside your range of vision as you settle down to the business of execution, so it is important to make your preliminary observations carefully and accurately.

Lengthen your bridge two or three inches and grasp the handle of the cue a corresponding distance behind your usual grip. Hit the ball slightly below center and go through it with a long, smooth stroke. The forearm does most of the work.

Steady! Hold your cue-tip in line until it touches the cloth four and a half to five inches beyond the point of contact. Don't be too eager to turn your head and see if the shot has counted. Remember, you must keep your mind and your eye rivetted to the first object ball until the stroke is completed.

Don't try to hit too hard. A long draw requires only slightly more force than a short one, but it needs every bit of wrist action and steadiness of nerve you can put into it.

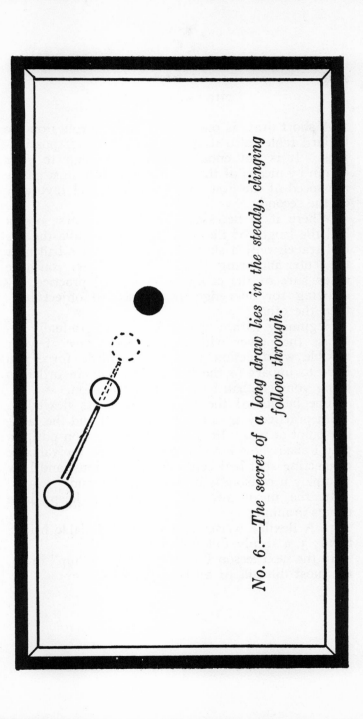

*No. 6.—The secret of a long draw lies in the steady, clinging follow through.*

# LESSON NO. 7

A short draw is one of the easiest strokes on the billiard table; also it contains the greatest possibilities. It is not enough merely to complete your carom by means of the short draw; you must gauge the speed of the first object ball and land favorably on the second.

Where it is necessary to drive the first object ball the length of the table and back, while the cue ball travels only a short distance, hit your ball near the center and bring it back slowly. After you have made sure of the count by continued practice, try drawing for one edge of the second object ball; then the other.

Beginning with a firm, bold stroke, gradually decrease the power without sacrificing any of your flexible wrist action and see how little force you have to impart to the first object ball, in order to bring your cue ball back to its destination.

The beauty of the short draw is its flexibility. With practice you can vary the speed and the landing point at will. In subsequent lessons on position play I shall show how the short draw is the valuable connecting shot between nursing positions, and how I employ it constantly in making a big run.

In the meantime, while practising keep these things in mind:

1. A flexible wrist; 2, a firm, dependable bridge hand; 3, a steady follow-through.

In the next lesson I shall explain the "nip" draw, the most difficult of all draw strokes.

*No. 7—(a)  Quick action on a short draw: strike the cue ball low.*

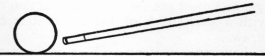

*(b)  Drawing for the upper edge; a short draw has great position possibilities.*

# LESSON NO. 8

This is the most difficult of all draw strokes. When your cue ball is so close to the first object ball that you have no room for an ordinary follow-through, and must put the downward action on your ball with a sharp flick of the wrist, it is called a 'nip' draw.

You have only half an inch or perhaps an inch to work in. Here is where the delicate wrist action is all important. Lengthen your bridge until your left hand is five or six inches away from the cue ball. This will give you more freedom of action.

The stroke is a sharp, upward swing of the cue. It must be firm and decisive. Make the cue-ball feel the sharp, downward thrust of the tip.

Here is the most valuable guide of all. To stop your cue from going too far through the ball, and thus fouling the stroke when it comes in contact with the object ball, bring the cue handle up sharply against the heel of your hand. Your hand will immediately check its course.

Practise this odd stroke. Snap your cue handle up against the heel of your hand a dozen times to get the "feel" of the action. Then try it with the cue ball only an inch from the object ball, and see how it solves the problem of that difficult, close position.

No. 8.—Secret of the "Nip" draw.

Stop your cue from going through too far by snapping the butt against the palm.

# LESSON NO. 9

## THE FOLLOW

In the follow shot the cue tip strikes the ball at center, or slightly above, and rises gradually as it goes through, producing over-spin. Its action is the reverse of the draw. Here again the wrist gives the final thrust to the cue-tip which determines the destiny of the shot, and as in the draw stroke the smooth flexible action of the wrist causes the tip to cling to the ivory surface until the stroke is complete. Likewise, it is the last half inch of the stroke that counts the most.

Your bridge hand should arch up slightly for this shot; but keep the finger tips and the heel of the hand firmly on the table. The handle of your cue should be kept low, as in the draw.

Keep your eye fixed on the first object ball as you go through the stroke; keep your cue firmly in line and as at the finish of the draw stroke, hold it for a second or two.

Your eye will play a mean trick on you in the follow shot unless you are careful. Both object balls are ahead and there is an almost irresistible impulse to transfer the gaze to the second ball at the instant the stroke is delivered. Don't do it! Many a follow shot has been missed because the player tried to look at both object balls at the same time. Get your aim first, as you make the preliminary waggle; know definitely where you must hit the first object ball; then go through the stroke steadily without transferring your gaze to the further ball.

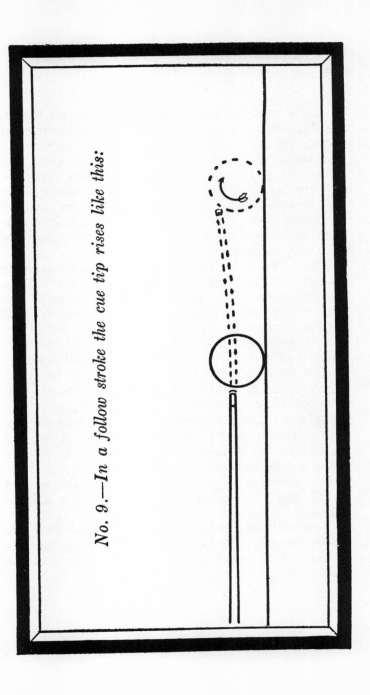

*No. 9.—In a follow stroke the cue tip rises like this:*

# LESSON NO. 10

## THE HALF FOLLOW

As the angle of the follow shot begins to widen, the top-spin on your cue ball exerts decreasing influence on the forward course of the balls. As you strike the first object ball further from the center, its receding circumference throws your cue ball further and further from its original course. Be careful; you are in a danger zone; the zone of the half-follow, that hybrid stroke which can produce such wonderful results in position, and yet is so easy to miss.

The half follow is deceptive. The angle is wide enough so that you could make the shot with a simple carom. But a thin shot would leave the first object ball behind and push the second ball further away with the cue ball between, hopelessly out of position. The problem is to take the first object ball along with you; hence the half-follow.

Aim near the center of the first ball, for your cue ball has a remarkable tendency to work out. As your cue-tip bites into the ivory give your ball a slight twist on the inside. That will hold the cue ball to its course and also speed the first object ball on its way, for it has a longer distance to travel and needs a little acceleration off the cushion.

Don't forget to go on through with the stroke! Don't stop your cue halfway, even if it is a half-follow.

You will need a lot of practice to calculate the angle correctly. It is practise well spent, for this is one of the most valuable position shots in the game.

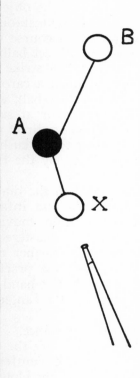

*No. 10.—The tricky half-follow; keep
your eye on A.*

# LESSON NO. 11

Now a word about billiard theory. The object of the game is to direct the cue ball against one of the object balls in such a way that its course when deflected, will lead it to the second object ball. In other words, you must make your ball strike both the others. That double click is called a carom.

The simplest form of carom is ball-to-ball, where the object balls lie so close together, or at such a favorable angle, that the cue ball takes a direct route from one to the other without resort to the cushions, or to any violent gyrations produced by the tip of the cue, such as underspin or massé.

Practise the simple carom shown in the diagram until your cue ball goes unerringly and infallibly from A to B. Then alter B's position, moving it slightly to the right. When you have mastered this angle at close range, place the balls further apart, still at a favorable angle, and continue practicing the simple carom until your eye and your hand have acquired the faculty of judging the angle instinctively.

Ivory is an elastic, resilient substance. It is "alive." Those sharp clicks you hear are the quick and lively reactions of the ivory circumference, contracting under the sharp impact of the blow, and quickly expanding to normal again.

It is the sensitiveness and elasticity of ivory that makes it possible to control the ball at will.

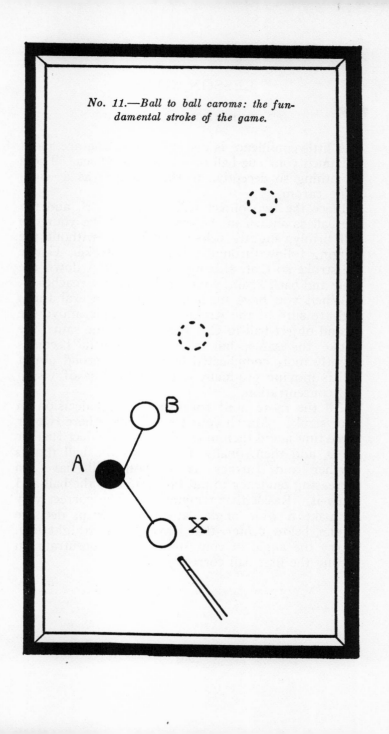

*No. 11.—Ball to ball caroms: the fun-damental stroke of the game.*

# LESSON NO. 12

A little confidence is needed here. You are about to launch your cue ball on an uncharted sea. There is nothing so deceptive to the beginner as a wide-angle carom.

Place the two object balls at A and B, and the cue ball as shown in the diagram. Strike your cue ball firmly, slightly below center, but without the clinging follow-through of the draw stroke. Gauge the stroke so that, although you knock A down the table and back again, your cue ball barely reaches B.

When you have made this carom several times and are sure of the stroke and the angle, move the second object ball to C. The angle is the same, the stroke the same, but now the problem becomes slightly more complicated because the second object ball is moving gradually out of your line of vision and concentration.

All the more need for firmness and decision in your stroke. March your cue ball over there two or three times, and then move the second object further to D, and then, finally, to E. As the ball moves further and further away, you will have an increasing tendency to put underspin on the ball and draw it. Resist that temptation. The correct way to make a wide angle carom is a crisp, decisive stroke, below center, that travels in a straight line. Carry the angle in your mind, and concentrate on hitting the first ball correctly.

No. 12.—*Wide angle carom played with firm center ball stroke.*

A

B

C

D

E

A

# LESSON NO. 13

Fifty years ago the famous old billiard players made most of their strokes with a lively cue ball. The cue ball did most of the travelling. Nowadays the height of professional skill is exemplified in the "dead ball."

What is a "dead ball"?

Place the balls as shown in the diagram. Strike the cue ball, X, with a firm stroke exactly in the center. Instead of going on through with the smooth, clinging action of the draw, let your cue tip "ease off" and seek the table bed three inches beyond the point of contact. The first object ball A is struck a small fraction of an inch to the right of center. That little deflection in its circumference is sufficient to send the cue ball travelling toward B.

Now a strange thing happens. Nearly all the initial force you put in the cue ball at the beginning of the stroke is transferred to A, propelling it down to the lower rail and back, while the cue ball becomes a dead ball, moving slowly, yet surely across the scant space of green cloth to B.

That is a perfect balk line stroke. Beginners, concentrating on the carom, will be inclined to strike A further around on its circumference, using a draw stroke to pull the cue ball back to B. Avoid that pitfall. Never mind whether you make the carom or not. Strike A full enough so that practically all the force of the cue is transferred to it.

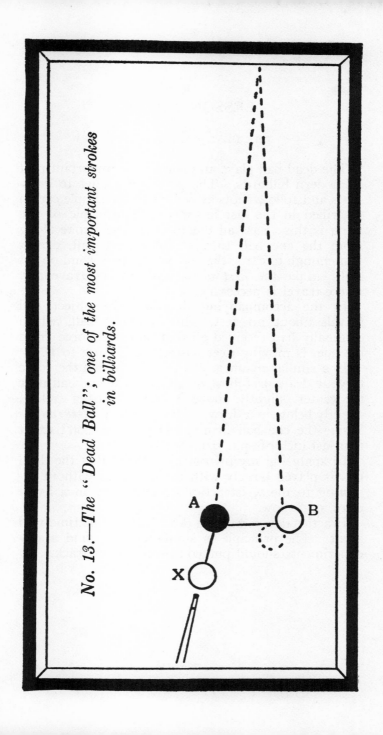

No. 13.—The "Dead Ball"; one of the most important strokes in billiards.

# LESSON NO. 14

The dead ball plays an enormously important part in modern billiards. The principle applies to draw shots and follow shots as well as to the simple carom described in the last lesson. The principle of the thing is this: Pass all the force of the stroke along from the cue ball to the first object ball, except just enough to carry the cue ball to the second object ball. Make the *first object ball* do the travelling, where travel is necessary.

In the accompanying diagram, the object ball travels about 20 feet, while the cue ball, which originally had received all that potential force from the cue, is moving over a scant six inches to B.

In a similar manner, you can tone down the force to your draw or follow by striking the cue ball near the center, slightly above in the case of a follow, slightly below in a draw. *Curb your follow-through!* Strike the cue ball firmly, sharply, but don't exact that last inch of spin from the ivory.

In analyzing my own stroke, I find that the dead ball is played largely with the forearm, without resorting to the wrist action so necessary in a lively draw or follow.

Practice devoted to the dead ball will be time well spent. The principle is simple enough, and a few experiments should put you on the right track.

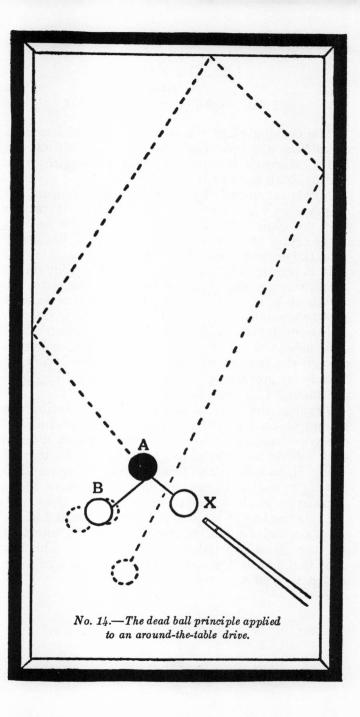

No. 14.—*The dead ball principle applied
to an around-the-table drive.*

# LESSON NO. 15

The cushion plays the part of a second baseman completing a double play. It catches a whirling cue ball, and sends it darting off at an angle to its destiny, with most of its speed intact.

I have arranged the balls in the accompanying diagram in what I call the "key shot." Here you have one object ball at, or near, the long side cushion at the center of the table. The cue ball, X, lies above it on the opposite side of the table.

It is possible to strike A at a certain point on its circumference and bring it back to complete the carom at B 1. It is possible to strike it at exactly the same point and bring it back to B2, B3, B4, B5, or B6. Such is the wide range of possibility on a ball-and-cushion shot. Now then, how is it possible to change the destiny of the cue ball nearly 10 feet? Simply by application of that cue magic, "English" accompanied by draw or follow.

Arrange the balls as in the diagram, placing the second object ball at B1. Hit the red half-full and cue your ball low and to the left and watch it come back. Now place the object ball at B6. Hit the red half full, as before and this time cue it high and to the right, and it comes out in a wide curve to its destination in the lower corner.

Place the ball at various positions, indicated in the diagram and familiarize yourself with the effect of English, draw and follow *off the cushion*. This key shot is the basis for a wide variety of strokes to be met with later on.

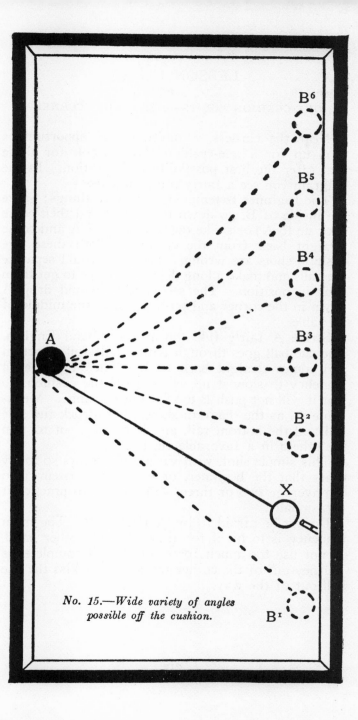

No. 15.—*Wide variety of angles possible off the cushion.*

# LESSON NO. 16

Near the corners, a multitude of opportunities crop up for a one-cushion shot. Look for those that offer the best possibilities of position. In the diagram you see a fairly common leave.

The beginner is tempted to do two things; graze the inside of B, go down to the rail and then come back up to A; or strike the thin edge of A and come straight back from the cushion. Both these one cushion shots are wrong. The first would separate the balls and make a long drive necessary to get them back in position. The second shot would drop A down in the corner and push B out in the middle of the table.

Strike A fairly full, top and left hand English. The cue ball goes through with a half-follow action and comes straight back to B. The "top" has a tendency to slow it up, coming off the cushion, so that it will not push B too far out of range. Meanwhile A, as the diagram shows, has struck the side rail and the bottom rail, and is coming out to join the others in a favorable cluster.

This simple shot, with variations, occurs so many times that the beginner, or even the amateur who can average two or three, will do well to practice it occasionally.

Do not be afraid to hit A fairly full. The main tendency is to hit it too thin. On the other hand, do not use too much force, or A will complete its journey out of the corner too soon and kiss the cue ball out of the way.

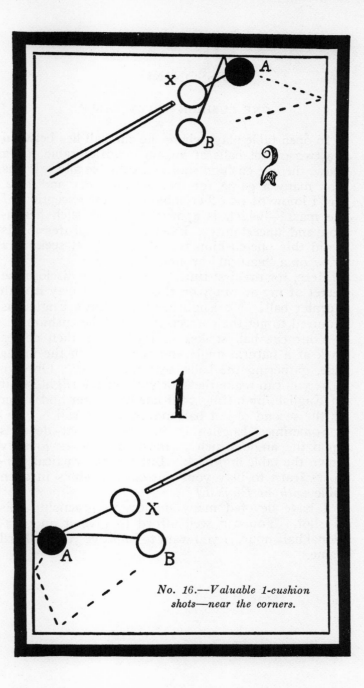

No. 16.—*Valuable 1-cushion shots—near the corners.*

# LESSON NO. 17

In open table play, where the cue ball lies between the two object balls at an angle unfavorable for a draw, the one cushion shot is a valuable ally. It has won many a game for me, both at 18.1 and 18.2. Yet I know of no other shot—with the exception of the massé—which is approached with such hesitation and uncertainty. Even the best professionals avoid this one-cushion try in open table, seeking a draw or a "natural" around the table.

Here, for the first time, I am going to disclose the secret of my accuracy on this stroke. I play it with a center ball! No English, or very little English is required to get the correct angle off the cushion.

Your cue ball strikes A fairly full, then comes back at a natural angle and strikes B on the upper side, gathering the balls near the corner. Observe this: you can make the shot without the slightest bit of English, by hitting your cue ball lower and lower as the second object ball moves up the rail.

Sometimes English is justified. That depends upon the angle which A must take in its journey down the table and back. But for all practical purposes learn to play your one-cushion shots in open table *without English!*

I have devoted many months to practising this X shot. You can well afford to give it an occasional half hour, if you want to improve your billiard game.

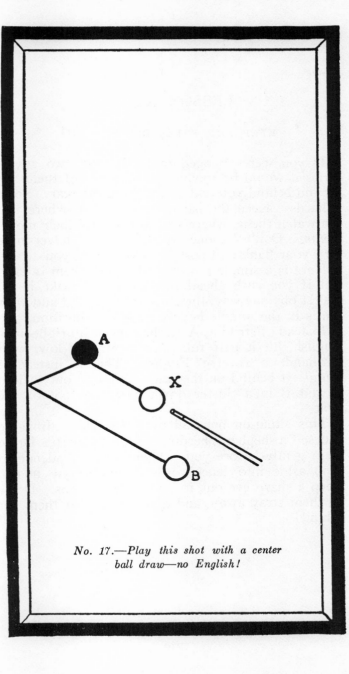

No. 17.—*Play this shot with a center
ball draw—no English!*

# LESSON NO. 18

If you were engaged in battle with two adversaries it would be foolhardy to let one of them slip around behind you and attack from the rear. So in billiards. Keep the balls ahead of you where you can watch them; where you can control their movements. Don't let one of those ivory adversaries turn your flank and post himself behind you.

Here is a simple illustration. The carom is easy. But if you rush ahead heedlessly and make it the easiest obvious way, the balls are scattered and your cue is in the middle hopelessly out of position.

Instead of striking A on the edge, with right-hand English, hit it half full. Cue your ball low, with left hand, or "reverse" English. Then A, instead of being left behind on the rail, will hurry out to join X and B in a cluster down near the foot of the table.

This situation bobs all over the table. Imagine yourself a shepherd, herding a flock of sheep. Drive them gently before you. They have a tendency to drop aside into fence corners, and grassy nooks. Keep a sharp eye out for these derelictions. Don't let them stray away, and don't let one of them get behind!

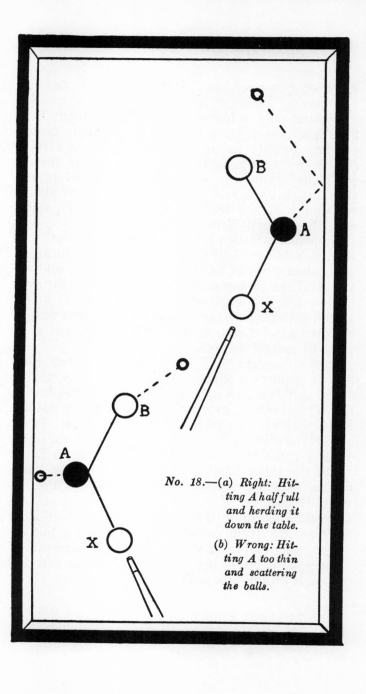

No. 18.—(a) Right: Hitting A half full and herding it down the table.

(b) Wrong: Hitting A too thin and scattering the balls.

# LESSON NO. 19

Theoretically, a billiard ball, struck without English, rebounds from a cushion at an angle corresponding exactly to its original course. Carrying this theory a little further and summoning the aid of plane geometry, a billiard ball striking two cushions, i. e., a side rail and an end rail, should rebound from the second on a line exactly parallel with its original course.

In actual practice this does not work out. As soon as a billiard ball strikes a cushion at an angle, it acquires a slight twist from the contact, and the action of the rubber also has a tendency to throw it slightly off. This slight twist takes effect on the second cushion with the result that instead of returning on a parallel course, the ball is thrown out at an angle of several degrees.

In the diagram, if X is struck without any English, it acquires a slight twist at A and this, taking effect at B, throws it back along the dotted line to D. Theoretically, its course would be along the line B—C which is parallel to the original course. If the cue ball be given a slight twist to the right, the angle of divergence is greater, throwing it over to E.

On the other hand, if reverse English be used, the cue ball will return *inside* the parallel line, as from B back to X again. *This is important:* a *natural* two-cushion shot (one struck without English) returns from the second cushion on a line diverging slightly from the parallel. The amount of divergence depends upon the speed of the ball and the angle on the first cushion.

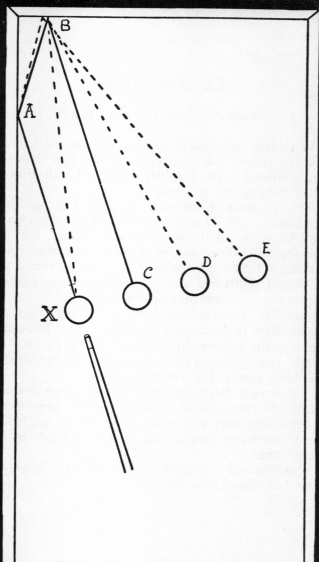

*No. 19.—Two cushion angles—natural,*
*and with English.*

# LESSON NO. 20

With two cushions to work on, your cue ball has a wide variety of courses. In the last lesson I demonstrated how English affects the destiny of a ball coming out of a corner.

The position illustrated in the diagram is a common variety of a two-cushion shot. Play softly off A, with left-hand English. Your cue ball doubles the corner and completes the carom on B, driving it into a cluster near A. Hit A fairly full, so that it will come straight out from the cushion, and not go gallivanting up the table.

Another two-cushion shot with good position possibilities is illustrated in Diagram 2. Instead of playing the carom direct from A to B, take the longer route around the corner, and you will gather the balls nicely for further caroms.

These two diagrams illustrate the most common forms of two-cushion "leaves." But there are so many situations where a two-cushion angle will yield favorable results that it is impossible to diagram them.

Practice will soon give you assurance in playing your ball around the corner.

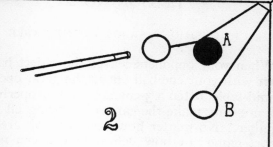

2

No. 20.—(2) Simple 2-cushion shot
"around the corner."

(1) Hit A fairly full, left
hand English.

1

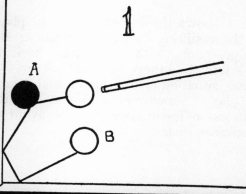

### 3 CUSHIONS—AROUND THE TABLE

When your opponent leaves the object balls wide apart with your cue ball out in the great open spaces of mid-table, often a 3-cushion shot, properly played, will not only make the carom but bring all the balls together. No matter how accurate you are in your "short game" or how delicately you can nurse the balls in a favorable position, you are at the mercy of your opponent if you fall down on open table play.

I should say 33⅓ per cent of open table play lies in choosing the right shot, 66⅔ in execution. Choose the shot that combines (1) certainty of counting and (2) the most favorable leave for the next shot.

The diagram gives a fairly common situation. Obviously the shot should be played off A, because B, favorably located in the corner, offers the greatest number of chances for completing the carom. Now this question arises; is it better to play behind A, striking the side rail before rounding the lower end of the table, or in front of A, directly to the end rail. The carom can be made either way, as far as X is concerned, but the results will be widely different with regard to the final location of A.

Diagram 1 shows the incorrect way to play the shot, and the resulting leave. Diagram 2 shows the correct procedure, with A marching back down the table to join the others near the corner.

This same situation arises again and again in open table play. Sometimes a kiss is threatened. In the next lesson I will show how to avoid these dangerous contingencies.

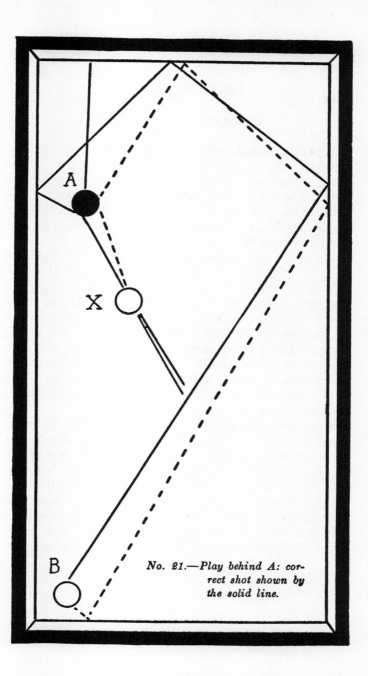

No. 21.—*Play behind A: correct shot shown by the solid line.*

# LESSON NO. 22

Here is a simple, effective way to ward off dangerous kiss-offs in open table play. Once you have decided upon your shot, make a mental diagram of
the course the first object ball will take. In the accompanying chart, it is clear, before the shot is
made that A will journey down to the lower rail and
return almost in a straight line.

Now estimate carefully at what point the cue
ball, X, will cross that path as it comes off the side
rail and starts on its journey around the table. That
danger point, indicated by the arrow, is the only
point, therefore, where the dreaded kiss may occur.

Having located that point definitely in your mind,
the problem now is to plan your stroke so that the
cue ball is safely past before A comes back from the
lower rail. X has a shorter distance to travel. But
if you strike A too full, or slow X up too much on
the cushion, you are in danger.

Play the shot briskly, with plenty of right hand
English, and you have nothing to worry about. In
all shots where a kiss is threatened; i. e., where the
cue ball crosses the path of the first object ball, lay
out that mental diagram and estimate carefully the
exact point of danger. Then either speed your cue
ball up to get out of the way, or slow it down, as
the case may be, to let A pass first. The same
principle applies in nearly all shots of this character.

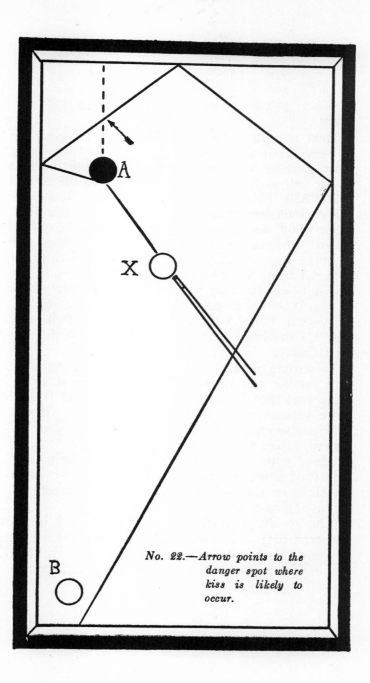

No. 22.—*Arrow points to the danger spot where kiss is likely to occur.*

# LESSON NO. 23

Here is a shot that requires a little imagination. Very often the opportunity arises of improving your position materially by drawing from the first object ball to the cushion, and thence to the second object ball, instead of direct ball to ball. Now there is a curious mental hazard connected with this shot. Your mind, accustomed to focussing on ivory, has a hard time readjusting its focus to the rubber rail.

In the diagram, X, the cue ball, must return to the side rail from A with under-spin and left-hand English sufficient to bring it sharply and decisively back to B. It would be easy enough to make a straight draw shot, from A to B without resort to the rail, but A's destination would be unfavorable for the next shot.

In settling yourself for this shot, mark the exact spot on the rail where your cue ball must strike. Keep that spot in mind. Focus on it as if B were there instead of further down the table. It will help you to regard that point on the rail as your objective, rather than the object ball, B.

Make your stroke smoothly and definitely, with plenty of English. Beware of a miscue, for of all the shots on the table where a miscue is threatened, this is the most likely.

The result, with A and B both herded in the corner, will justify your concentration. There are scores of shots where drawing off the rail will help you. Watch for them and play them courageously.

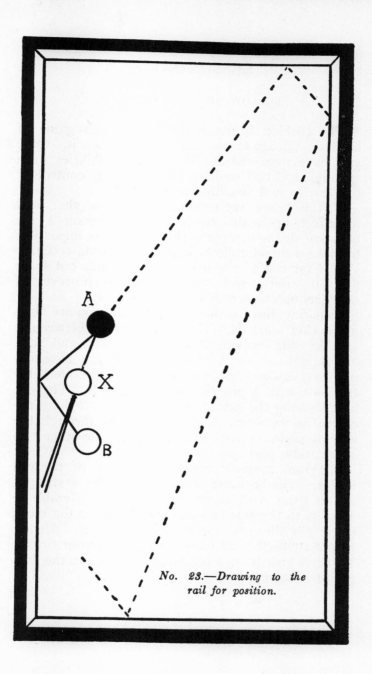

*No. 23.—Drawing to the rail for position.*

# LESSON NO. 24

The cushion is a valuable ally in this game of billiards. Learn to use it and depend upon it. Once you have mastered the intricate possibilities of a spinning cue ball striking the rail, your control of the ivories will steadily improve.

In this lesson we consider the follow shot, and its effect upon the cushion. In diagram 1 the balls are strung along the side rail. It is impossible to make a direct follow shot, for A would certainly kiss B far out of the way on its journey out from the rail. Between B and the cushion, however, is space enough to permit the passage of A.

In taking aim for this shot, imagine you are playing pocket billiards. The narrow space between B and the side cushion is a corner pocket, and your object is to drive A into it. Once you have determined upon your aim for this objective, play the shot with high, right-hand English. The cue ball, striking the rail spins down and completes the carom on B, while A, having passed through the narrow pocket, comes back and joins the other two in favorable position.

Diagram 2 shows another variation of the rail follow. The beginner is tempted to play a straight carom from A to B, but it is greatly preferable to drive A to the side rail and thence across the table, keeping it ahead of you in the short table. Always aim to strike the rail before completing your carom. This will kick B out a bit, and greatly lessen the danger of a line-up.

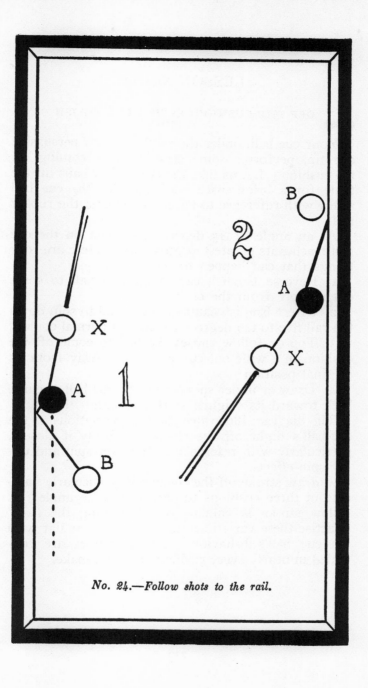

No. 24.—*Follow shots to the rail.*

# LESSON NO. 25

Your cue ball, under the influence of a persuasive cue tip, performs some strange feats coming off the cushion. Let us take the two object balls off the table for a brief space, and consider the cue ball solely with reference to its action against the rubber rail.

At an angle of 45 degrees the twist on the cue ball reaches its greatest effectiveness. Here are four things that can happen to it:

1. Reverse English causes the cue ball to come out sharply from the cushion;

2. Direct English causes the cue ball to spin down the rail five to ten degrees beyond its normal course;

3. Top or follow causes the ball to come off the cushion in a wide out-curve, tending away from its original position;

4. Draw or under-spin causes the cue ball to curve back toward its original starting point.

The diagram illustrates the four variations of the cue-ball's flight off the cushion. Study it closely, particularly with reference to the over-spin and under-spin effects.

A draw stroke off the cushion is particularly valuable in three cushions to correct a false angle. A follow stroke is valuable for "hugging the rail." Practise these variations until you are familiar with the cue ball's behavior. The principles are concealed in nearly every cushion shot you make.

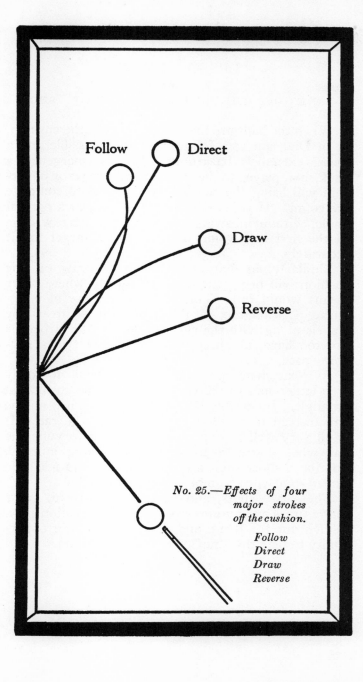

Follow Direct

Draw

Reverse

No. 25.—*Effects of four major strokes off the cushion.*

*Follow*
*Direct*
*Draw*
*Reverse*

# LESSON NO. 26

When the balls are lined up parallel to the cushion, as in Diagram 1, a follow shot is impossible and a massé extremely hazardous. In this emergency, a bank shot, played to the cushion with draw, or under-spin will bring the cue ball sharply out to complete the count. If you were to try the bank at a natural angle, without drawing your ball, the narrow edge of the first ball would be too small a target to hit accurately.

Similarly, in diagram 2, a sharp draw off the cushion will bring cue ball out quickly where other means would fail. This shot is very useful in securing position, too, for the object ball, A, invariably travels along with the cue ball, and if the stroke be not too hard, all three will come to rest in a narrow space.

A great many players find it difficult to apply true under-spin to the ball going into the cushion at an angle. Invariably they try to put English on the ball instead to facilitate its course off the rail. It is all very well to apply direct English to your cue ball when you have to send it on a long journey, but for a short shot, a center ball with just a little under-spin will accomplish the best results.

These two shots, and variations of them, occur many times as you improve your close position play. Watch out for them, and don't overlook an opportunity to play this "nip" shot off the cushion.

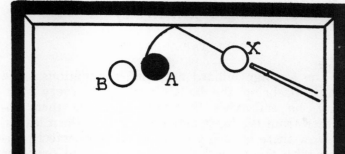

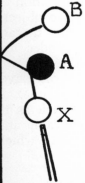

*No. 26.—Effects of a sharp
draw stroke off the
cushion.*

# LESSON NO. 27

The average billiard amateur is ambitious. He wants to bring the balls together on every shot. Nay, he endeavors heroically to bring them together from the most impossible and forlorn leaves.

Now there is such a thing as having perfect position with the three balls widely scattered over the table. And there are many bad positions in which the three balls are very close together.

Consider the situation in diagram 1. The carom is easy. X can be made to strike both A and B with a simple carom. But how can it be played to yield the best results? The novice, seeing a favorable angle for A around the end of the table, tries to get them together on the next shot. And there he makes a great mistake.

Strike A hard enough to send it over in the corner. Play your cue ball with left hand twist so that it will carom above B and come to rest a few inches away. Now you are in perfect position for a gather shot in the corner, and your carom is one of the easiest on the table.

Watch out for these "open table position" shots. No matter how widely spread the two object balls, if your cue ball is on the outside, and the angle is favorable, you can keep them under control. Don't try to put them "under a hat" every time you shoot. Time enough for that when you have mastered all the elemental points of the game. In the meantime, watch for opportunities such as that illustrated in the accompanying diagram, and you will be surprised at the frequency with which they occur.

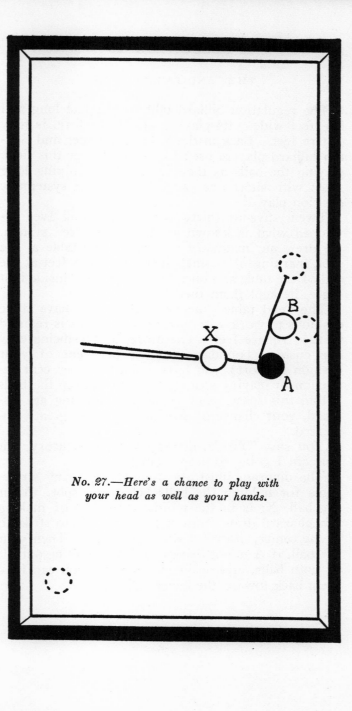

No. 27.—*Here's a chance to play with your head as well as your hands.*

# LESSON NO. 28

The regulation billiard table is ten feet long and five feet wide. Its playing area, therefore, is fifty square feet. Back in the days of Garnier and Sexton billiard players used to romp all over this field, playing the balls as they found them, mixing long shots with short ones and disregarding systematic position play.

Twenty-five or thirty years ago Frank Ives developed what is known as the "end table" system. He drew an imaginary line across the table at the spot, marking off a small space $2\frac{1}{2}$ by 5 feet at the end of the table and once he got the balls inside that space, he kept them there.

The "end table" theory is this: you have three cushions to work with, your playing area is reduced to $12\frac{1}{2}$ square feet. Therefore, by sacrificing only one cushion boundary (or 25 per cent of your cushion support) you have gained 75 per cent reduction of playing space. If you can keep the balls within this space, your chances of missing are lessened, your chance of scoring big runs, greatly increased.

You say, "That's all very well as a theory, but how am I going to keep them there?"

The diagram illustrates one of the many stratagems for holding the balls below the spot. Your cue ball, X, is in the middle. Instead of making a haphazard draw from A to B, aiming to strike B in the center, draw for the outer edge. Then your cue ball, if A is not driven too hard, will be outside of both balls, and on your next shot you can herd them back toward the lower rail.

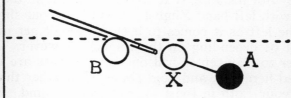

Avoid the great open spaces!

No. 28.—*Avoid the great open spaces!*

LANDING ON THE SECOND BALL—THE FINAL TWIST

When a billiard player has developed his game to the point where he can make a wide variety of shots, play position fairly well, and control the cue ball off the cushion, his further progress depends almost entirely on one thing—*landing on the second ball.*

In the last lesson we had an illustration of this principle, drawing for the outer edge of the second object ball instead of for its center. In the accompanying diagram is another similar case. The shot is a follow. Any amateur could make the carom nine or ten times out of ten. But here's the point: if you strike B on the inside and kick it out toward the open table, your next shot is almost sure to be a long drive with chances of losing control.

On the other hand, if you play the follow so that X strikes B on the outside (just above center, not out on the edge) your cue ball will be in favorable position to keep them in control, regardless of where A stops on its return journey.

In playing for close position on the second ball, the English on your cue ball plays an important rôle. For instance, if X strikes B exactly in the center, with left-hand English, it will twist out slightly to the left as it comes to a stop. Don't get in the habit of depending on the English, however. It is better to play center ball on shots such as are illustrated herewith, and land accurately, rather than to put your faith in twist to bring you around.

In short follows and draws you can nearly always send your cue ball to the right or left of the second object ball. Choose the most advantageous position and land accordingly.

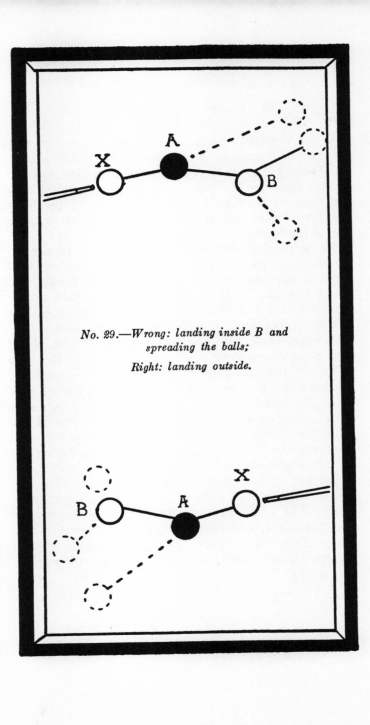

No. 29.—*Wrong: landing inside B and
spreading the balls;*

*Right: landing outside.*

# LESSON NO. 30

When the two object balls are close together and the cue ball nearby, it is possible to make a very satisfactory cluster of caroms without driving any of the balls to the rail. The "nurse position" in balk line, of course, is valuable only when the balls are out in the unrestricted center panel, or astride one of the lines.

Be careful on your first shot! Don't spoil a good position by your eagerness to count one or two isolated caroms. Strike the first ball fairly full —but not hard. Now here is an important point. The cue ball should always pass the center of the second object ball; in other words, get outside it. Now come back, with the same delicate stroke, being careful again on your return journey to hit the first ball quite full and pass the center of the second.

There are a thousand delicate variations of this shot. Experiment! Try right and left English. Put a little drag on your ball as it crosses the face of the other two. By observation and practice, you will soon acquire an instinctive knowledge of the exacting requirements of the nurse.

Let me again emphasize the importance of going slowly on your first shot or two. There is plenty of time. The balls have nowhere else to go. Make that first shot correctly and others are sure to follow. Presently, when you have acquired the "tempo" of the nurse, you can click them off rapidly and easily.

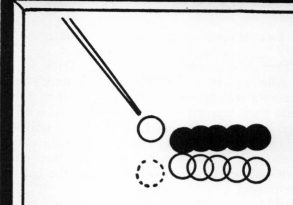

*No. 30.—Play softly, without English, just passing center of the second ball.*

# LESSON NO. 31

## THE MASSÉ—MAKING THE BRIDGE

The French discovered the massé. Back in the time of Albert Garnier, and even in Vignaux's early days, the shot was played with a good deal of force, and while they learned to count effectively with it, often the balls were knocked out of close position. It was Jacob Schaefer the elder who first developed the velvet-stroked massé which gives a sharp curve to the cue-ball, counts lightly and leaves the balls in close formation.

The bridge is all important. The left hand should be planted firmly on the table so that the cue will have solid support as it goes into the ball. There are two orthodox methods of making a massé bridge. One is to make a tripod of the last three fingers of the left hand, with the little finger firmly planted behind, the ring finger forming the left support, and the middle finger under the palm to the right. The fore finger is curled up to lend guidance and support to the cue.

Another bridge—used by Horemans and Schaefer —is made with the fingers spread out fanwise, and palm of the hand turned in toward the ball. Adopt the bridge that best suits your hand, but be sure it is firm and unwavering. There is no other shot where accuracy and control depend so largely upon the left hand.

The cue may be held with the thumb of the right hand down; i. e., without shifting the normal position of the hand, or held between the thumb and fingers with the thumb uppermost. Here again the player must try both styles and choose that which gives best results.

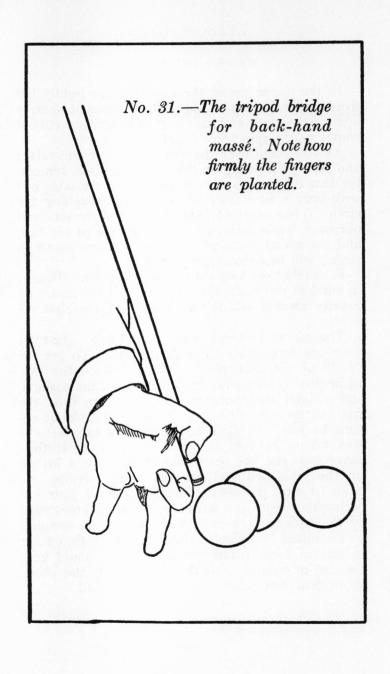

*No. 31.—The tripod bridge for back-hand massé. Note how firmly the fingers are planted.*

# LESSON NO. 32

In the massé stroke, the cue-tip drops lightly but firmly near the top of the ball, squeezes it sharply against the cloth and causes it to describe a curved course as the spin takes effect.

As you stand over the ball, with your cue raised and the tip focussing on the curved surface, remember that the ivory sphere is resting on the table bed with only a tiny fraction of its area touching the cloth. That point of contact is, to all intents and purposes, a pin point, yet all the weight of the ball, and the added force of the blow you are about to strike, will be concentrated there.

Remember the location of that pin point. Bear it in mind as you make the shot, for it is the center of gravity around which the destiny of the shot revolves.

The massé requires very little force. Just let your cue drop easily through the ball. To get the "feel" of the shot, place a single ball on the rail, make your bridge with the left hand on the cushion, and without attempting to make a carom, force the cue ball up the rail a few inches and make it return to you. Practice this until you can feel the spin taking hold of the ball on every shot; then move your cue ball out in the table, make a bridge on the table bed and practice there, varying the point of aim, the speed, force, etc., until your experiments supply you with the elemental knowledge of the stroke. The cue-tip should, on no account, be permitted to follow through to the cloth, except in certain force massé strokes. You should keep the cue in control with the right hand, and check its descent just before the cloth is reached.

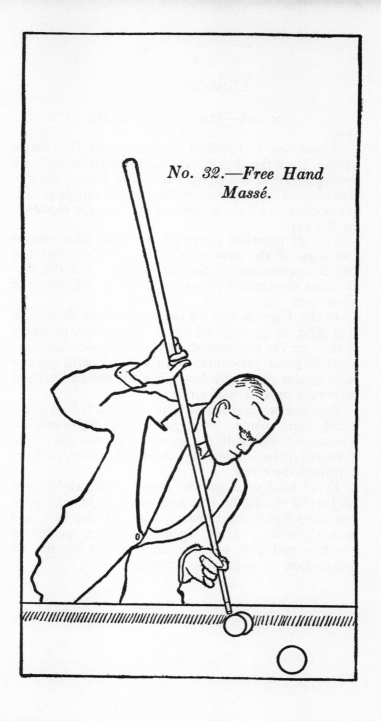

No. 32.—*Free Hand Massé.*

# LESSON NO. 33

There are a hundred variations of the massé stroke, from the slow curve that takes effect eighteen inches away to the sharp curve that brings the cue ball around in a narrow radius. One simple principle applies to all those varying curves: the elevation of the cue.

For all practical purposes, you can take aim at the edge of the first object ball, and hit your cue ball in approximately the same place. But the factor that determines the curve itself, is the angle of your cue.

In the diagram you see the cue at three elevations. The first, at an angle of about 45 degrees, produces a slow curve; the second, at a greater elevation, results in a sharper curve, and the third, with the cue held almost perpendicular brings the cue ball around in a very narrow half circle.

Remember this; massé shots are played on practically one plane, as regards the right-and-left variation. But it is the elevation of the cue; i. e., forward or back from the player's shoulder, that determines the curve.

Don't hold your cue too firmly. The right hand and wrist should be free and supple. Just let your cue drop lightly and sharply through the ball, and watch results. Here again, plodding, persistent practice will give you the touch as no amount of instruction or observation can do.

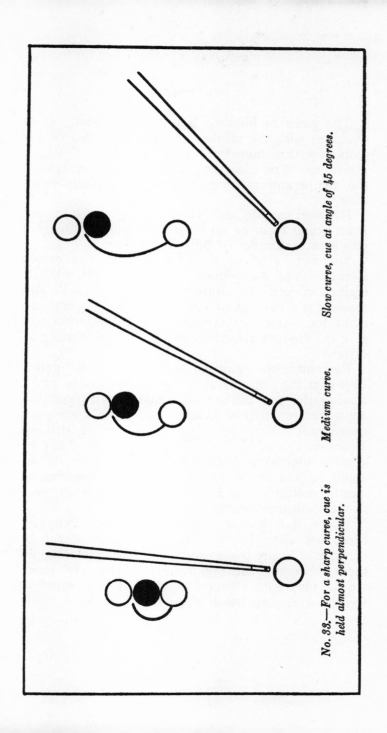

No. 33.—For a sharp curve, cue is held almost perpendicular.    Medium curve.    Slow curve, cue at angle of 45 degrees.

# LESSON NO. 34

The game of billiards is a battle of wits. Once equipped with the strokes and fundamentals of the game you are launched on a contest of skill and ingenuity. You must pit your craftsmanship against the temperamental perverseness of rolling ivory balls.

No man can do another's thinking for him, but I am going to draw on my own experience to give you some examples of billiard strategy.

Diagram 1 gives common leave. The carom is easy. You can glance off A to B without half trying, or you can draw back from B to A and make it 9 times out of ten. Position prospects are good, too. But the question arises: which shot will give me the best arrangement for a large number of caroms?

Remember the principle of the "end table" game. Slip past the edge of A and past the inside of B, leaving the cue ball on the outside, with position approximately that of Diagram 2. Now study your shot again. You have an easy draw shot, driving B across the table. In taking your aim, don't be content merely with completing the carom on A. Land on the upper side, as shown in diagram 3, and no matter where B stops, you are in good position to continue the run.

Every shot has strategic possibilities. No two shots are alike but all have certain principles in common. Study these principles, and learn to apply them whenever the opportunity offers. In other words, play with all the resources of your mind as well as with your hands and eyes.

*No. 34.—Watch for an op-
portunity to drop
softly through the
balls instead of
driving or spread-
ing them.*

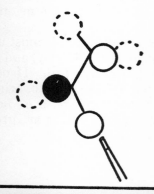

# LESSON NO. 35

Here we come to the most delicate, exacting system of stroke control in the game of billiards—the *balk line nurse*. George Butler Sutton was the first to perfect it; all professionals rely heavily upon it in scoring big runs.

When the object balls are close together on the line it is always possible, with a few "nurse" strokes to get them approximately in the position shown in Diagram 1. The problem is to drive the first object ball A to the side rail and out again to join the others an inch or so to the right, cue ball X meanwhile having counted softly against B.

The secret lies in the short drive of A, and in accurately judging the angle of its return.

English applied to the cue ball is transferred, with opposite effect, to the first object ball. It is possible, therefore, to deflect A's angle two or three degrees to the right or left at will. Aim to bring it back so that it will lightly kiss the cue ball *not the second object ball!* The tendency of most amateurs is to throw A too far to the right, so that it either kisses B away, or hides in a line-up on the far side of B.

The cue ball's rôle is important too. It must move over very gently so as not to block B away, and then block A on its journey out from the rail. If necessary, put a slight draw on the cue ball to bring it outside of B, because if it lands inside, i. e., nearer the rail, the chances of favorable position are greatly lessened.

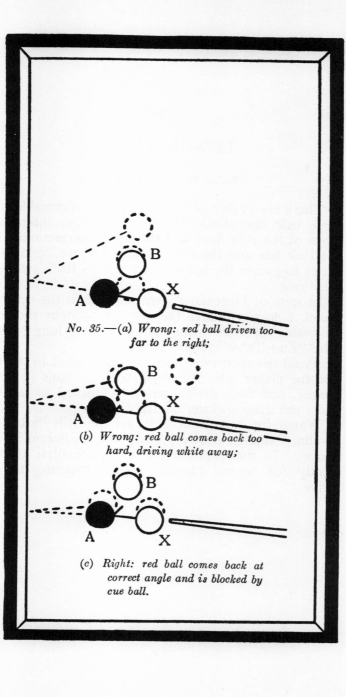

No. 35.—(a) *Wrong: red ball driven too far to the right;*

(b) *Wrong: red ball comes back too hard, driving white away;*

(c) *Right: red ball comes back at correct angle and is blocked by cue ball.*

# LESSON NO. 36

There are twelve points on the table favorable to close balk line play. These are the four intersections of the balk lines and the eight intersections of the balk line and the rail. Watch out for opportunities to gather the balls at any one of these twelve positions.

In spite of Horemans' great success in the center panel, I do not believe the average amateur should cultivate that space in the hope of making long runs. The "End Table" theory is best.

Avoid the corners. There is much grief in store for the player who tries to gather the balls in the corner, and then finds himself compelled to drive them out after making one shot.

Watch for opportunities to get the balls "astride the line," that is, close together, but in different balk spaces. In this position you can manipulate them gently for several caroms, before resorting to a drive.

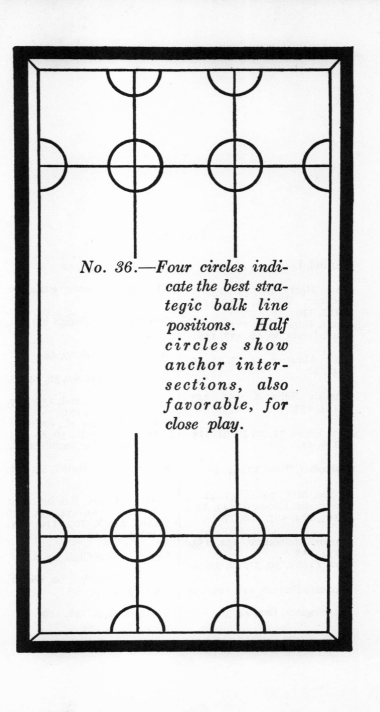

No. 36.—*Four circles indicate the best strategic balk line positions. Half circles show anchor intersections, also favorable, for close play.*

# INDEX

A CATALOGUE OF SELECTED DOVER BOOKS
IN ALL FIELDS OF INTEREST

# A CATALOGUE OF SELECTED DOVER BOOKS
## IN ALL FIELDS OF INTEREST

AMERICA'S OLD MASTERS, James T. Flexner. Four men emerged unexpectedly from provincial 18th century America to leadership in European art: Benjamin West, J. S. Copley, C. R. Peale, Gilbert Stuart. Brilliant coverage of lives and contributions. Revised, 1967 edition. 69 plates. 365pp. of text.

21806-6 Paperbound $3.00

FIRST FLOWERS OF OUR WILDERNESS: AMERICAN PAINTING, THE COLONIAL PERIOD, James T. Flexner. Painters, and regional painting traditions from earliest Colonial times up to the emergence of Copley, West and Peale Sr., Foster, Gustavus Hesselius, Feke, John Smibert and many anonymous painters in the primitive manner. Engaging presentation, with 162 illustrations. xxii + 368pp.

22180-6 Paperbound $3.50

THE LIGHT OF DISTANT SKIES: AMERICAN PAINTING, 1760-1835, James T. Flexner. The great generation of early American painters goes to Europe to learn and to teach: West, Copley, Gilbert Stuart and others. Allston, Trumbull, Morse; also contemporary American painters—primitives, derivatives, academics—who remained in America. 102 illustrations. xiii + 306pp. 22179-2 Paperbound $3.50

A HISTORY OF THE RISE AND PROGRESS OF THE ARTS OF DESIGN IN THE UNITED STATES, William Dunlap. Much the richest mine of information on early American painters, sculptors, architects, engravers, miniaturists, etc. The only source of information for scores of artists, the major primary source for many others. Unabridged reprint of rare original 1834 edition, with new introduction by James T. Flexner, and 394 new illustrations. Edited by Rita Weiss. 6⅝ x 9⅝.

21695-0, 21696-9, 21697-7 Three volumes, Paperbound $15.00

EPOCHS OF CHINESE AND JAPANESE ART, Ernest F. Fenollosa. From primitive Chinese art to the 20th century, thorough history, explanation of every important art period and form, including Japanese woodcuts; main stress on China and Japan, but Tibet, Korea also included. Still unexcelled for its detailed, rich coverage of cultural background, aesthetic elements, diffusion studies, particularly of the historical period. 2nd, 1913 edition. 242 illustrations. lii + 439pp. of text.

20364-6, 20365-4 Two volumes, Paperbound $6.00

THE GENTLE ART OF MAKING ENEMIES, James A. M. Whistler. Greatest wit of his day deflates Oscar Wilde, Ruskin, Swinburne; strikes back at inane critics, exhibitions, art journalism; aesthetics of impressionist revolution in most striking form. Highly readable classic by great painter. Reproduction of edition designed by Whistler. Introduction by Alfred Werner. xxxvi + 334pp.

21875-9 Paperbound $3.00

VISUAL ILLUSIONS: THEIR CAUSES, CHARACTERISTICS, AND APPLICATIONS, Matthew Luckiesh. Thorough description and discussion of optical illusion, geometric and perspective, particularly; size and shape distortions, illusions of color, of motion; natural illusions; use of illusion in art and magic, industry, etc. Most useful today with op art, also for classical art. Scores of effects illustrated. Introduction by William H. Ittleson. 100 illustrations. xxi + 252pp.

21530-X Paperbound $2.00

A HANDBOOK OF ANATOMY FOR ART STUDENTS, Arthur Thomson. Thorough, virtually exhaustive coverage of skeletal structure, musculature, etc. Full text, supplemented by anatomical diagrams and drawings and by photographs of undraped figures. Unique in its comparison of male and female forms, pointing out differences of contour, texture, form. 211 figures, 40 drawings, 86 photographs. xx + 459pp. 5⅜ x 8⅜.

21163-0 Paperbound $3.50

150 MASTERPIECES OF DRAWING, Selected by Anthony Toney. Full page reproductions of drawings from the early 16th to the end of the 18th century, all beautifully reproduced: Rembrandt, Michelangelo, Dürer, Fragonard, Urs, Graf, Wouwerman, many others. First-rate browsing book, model book for artists. xviii + 150pp. 8⅜ x 11¼.

21032-4 Paperbound $2.50

THE LATER WORK OF AUBREY BEARDSLEY, Aubrey Beardsley. Exotic, erotic, ironic masterpieces in full maturity: Comedy Ballet, Venus and Tannhauser, Pierrot, Lysistrata, Rape of the Lock, Savoy material, Ali Baba, Volpone, etc. This material revolutionized the art world, and is still powerful, fresh, brilliant. With *The Early Work*, all Beardsley's finest work. 174 plates, 2 in color. xiv + 176pp. 8⅛ x 11.

21817-1 Paperbound $3.00

DRAWINGS OF REMBRANDT, Rembrandt van Rijn. Complete reproduction of fabulously rare edition by Lippmann and Hofstede de Groot, completely reedited, updated, improved by Prof. Seymour Slive, Fogg Museum. Portraits, Biblical sketches, landscapes, Oriental types, nudes, episodes from classical mythology—All Rembrandt's fertile genius. Also selection of drawings by his pupils and followers. "Stunning volumes," *Saturday Review*. 550 illustrations. lxxviii + 552pp. 9⅛ x 12¼.

21485-0, 21486-9 Two volumes, Paperbound $10.00

THE DISASTERS OF WAR, Francisco Goya. One of the masterpieces of Western civilization—83 etchings that record Goya's shattering, bitter reaction to the Napoleonic war that swept through Spain after the insurrection of 1808 and to war in general. Reprint of the first edition, with three additional plates from Boston's Museum of Fine Arts. All plates facsimile size. Introduction by Philip Hofer, Fogg Museum. v + 97pp. 9⅜ x 8¼.

21872-4 Paperbound $2.00

GRAPHIC WORKS OF ODILON REDON. Largest collection of Redon's graphic works ever assembled: 172 lithographs, 28 etchings and engravings, 9 drawings. These include some of his most famous works. All the plates from *Odilon Redon: oeuvre graphique complet,* plus additional plates. New introduction and caption translations by Alfred Werner. 209 illustrations. xxvii + 209pp. 9⅛ x 12¼.

21966-8 Paperbound $4.50

DESIGN BY ACCIDENT; A BOOK OF "ACCIDENTAL EFFECTS" FOR ARTISTS AND DESIGNERS, James F. O'Brien. Create your own unique, striking, imaginative effects by "controlled accident" interaction of materials: paints and lacquers, oil and water based paints, splatter, crackling materials, shatter, similar items. Everything you do will be different; first book on this limitless art, so useful to both fine artist and commercial artist. Full instructions. 192 plates showing "accidents," 8 in color. viii + 215pp. 8⅜ x 11¼.                                     21942-9 Paperbound $3.75

THE BOOK OF SIGNS, Rudolf Koch. Famed German type designer draws 493 beautiful symbols: religious, mystical, alchemical, imperial, property marks, runes, etc. Remarkable fusion of traditional and modern. Good for suggestions of timelessness, smartness, modernity. Text. vi + 104pp. 6⅛ x 9¼.
                                                      20162-7 Paperbound $1.25

HISTORY OF INDIAN AND INDONESIAN ART, Ananda K. Coomaraswamy. An unabridged republication of one of the finest books by a great scholar in Eastern art. Rich in descriptive material, history, social backgrounds; Sunga reliefs, Rajput paintings, Gupta temples, Burmese frescoes, textiles, jewelry, sculpture, etc. 400 photos. viii + 423pp. 6⅜ x 9¾.                          21436-2 Paperbound $5.00

PRIMITIVE ART, Franz Boas. America's foremost anthropologist surveys textiles, ceramics, woodcarving, basketry, metalwork, etc.; patterns, technology, creation of symbols, style origins. All areas of world, but very full on Northwest Coast Indians. More than 350 illustrations of baskets, boxes, totem poles, weapons, etc. 378 pp.
                                                      20025-6 Paperbound $3.00

THE GENTLEMAN AND CABINET MAKER'S DIRECTOR, Thomas Chippendale. Full reprint (third edition, 1762) of most influential furniture book of all time, by master cabinetmaker. 200 plates, illustrating chairs, sofas, mirrors, tables, cabinets, plus 24 photographs of surviving pieces. Biographical introduction by N. Bienenstock. vi + 249pp. 9⅞ x 12¾.                          21601-2 Paperbound $4.00

AMERICAN ANTIQUE FURNITURE, Edgar G. Miller, Jr. The basic coverage of all American furniture before 1840. Individual chapters cover type of furniture— clocks, tables, sideboards, etc.—chronologically, with inexhaustible wealth of data. More than 2100 photographs, all identified, commented on. Essential to all early American collectors. Introduction by H. E. Keyes. vi + 1106pp. 7⅞ x 10¾.
                        21599-7, 21600-4 Two volumes, Paperbound $11.00

PENNSYLVANIA DUTCH AMERICAN FOLK ART, Henry J. Kauffman. 279 photos, 28 drawings of tulipware, Fraktur script, painted tinware, toys, flowered furniture, quilts, samplers, hex signs, house interiors, etc. Full descriptive text. Excellent for tourist, rewarding for designer, collector. Map. 146pp. 7⅞ x 10¾.
                                                      21205-X Paperbound $2.50

EARLY NEW ENGLAND GRAVESTONE RUBBINGS, Edmund V. Gillon, Jr. 43 photographs, 226 carefully reproduced rubbings show heavily symbolic, sometimes macabre early gravestones, up to early 19th century. Remarkable early American primitive art, occasionally strikingly beautiful; always powerful. Text. xxvi + 207pp. 8⅜ x 11¼.                                      21380-3 Paperbound $3.50

ALPHABETS AND ORNAMENTS, Ernst Lehner. Well-known pictorial source for decorative alphabets, script examples, cartouches, frames, decorative title pages, calligraphic initials, borders, similar material. 14th to 19th century, mostly European. Useful in almost any graphic arts designing, varied styles. 750 illustrations. 256pp. 7 x 10.
21905-4 Paperbound $4.00

PAINTING: A CREATIVE APPROACH, Norman Colquhoun. For the beginner simple guide provides an instructive approach to painting: major stumbling blocks for beginner; overcoming them, technical points; paints and pigments; oil painting; watercolor and other media and color. New section on "plastic" paints. Glossary. Formerly *Paint Your Own Pictures*. 221pp.
22000-1 Paperbound $1.75

THE ENJOYMENT AND USE OF COLOR, Walter Sargent. Explanation of the relations between colors themselves and between colors in nature and art, including hundreds of little-known facts about color values, intensities, effects of high and low illumination, complementary colors. Many practical hints for painters, references to great masters. 7 color plates, 29 illustrations. x + 274pp.
20944-X Paperbound $2.75

THE NOTEBOOKS OF LEONARDO DA VINCI, compiled and edited by Jean Paul Richter. 1566 extracts from original manuscripts reveal the full range of Leonardo's versatile genius: all his writings on painting, sculpture, architecture, anatomy, astronomy, geography, topography, physiology, mining, music, etc., in both Italian and English, with 186 plates of manuscript pages and more than 500 additional drawings. Includes studies for the Last Supper, the lost Sforza monument, and other works. Total of xlvii + 866pp. 7⅞ x 10¾.
22572-0, 22573-9 Two volumes, Paperbound $11.00

MONTGOMERY WARD CATALOGUE OF 1895. Tea gowns, yards of flannel and pillow-case lace, stereoscopes, books of gospel hymns, the New Improved Singer Sewing Machine, side saddles, milk skimmers, straight-edged razors, high-button shoes, spittoons, and on and on . . . listing some 25,000 items, practically all illustrated. Essential to the shoppers of the 1890's, it is our truest record of the spirit of the period. Unaltered reprint of Issue No. 57, Spring and Summer 1895. Introduction by Boris Emmet. Innumerable illustrations. xiii + 624pp. 8½ x 11⅝.
22377-9 Paperbound $6.95

THE CRYSTAL PALACE EXHIBITION ILLUSTRATED CATALOGUE (LONDON, 1851). One of the wonders of the modern world—the Crystal Palace Exhibition in which all the nations of the civilized world exhibited their achievements in the arts and sciences—presented in an equally important illustrated catalogue. More than 1700 items pictured with accompanying text—ceramics, textiles, cast-iron work, carpets, pianos, sleds, razors, wall-papers, billiard tables, beehives, silverware and hundreds of other artifacts—represent the focal point of Victorian culture in the Western World. Probably the largest collection of Victorian decorative art ever assembled—indispensable for antiquarians and designers. Unabridged republication of the Art-Journal Catalogue of the Great Exhibition of 1851, with all terminal essays. New introduction by John Gloag, F.S.A. xxxiv + 426pp. 9 x 12.
22503-8 Paperbound $5.00

A History of Costume, Carl Köhler. Definitive history, based on surviving pieces of clothing primarily, and paintings, statues, etc. secondarily. Highly readable text, supplemented by 594 illustrations of costumes of the ancient Mediterranean peoples, Greece and Rome, the Teutonic prehistoric period; costumes of the Middle Ages, Renaissance, Baroque, 18th and 19th centuries. Clear, measured patterns are provided for many clothing articles. Approach is practical throughout. Enlarged by Emma von Sichart. 464pp. 21030-8 Paperbound $3.50.

Oriental Rugs, Antique and Modern, Walter A. Hawley. A complete and authoritative treatise on the Oriental rug—where they are made, by whom and how, designs and symbols, characteristics in detail of the six major groups, how to distinguish them and how to buy them. Detailed technical data is provided on periods, weaves, warps, wefts, textures, sides, ends and knots, although no technical background is required for an understanding. 11 color plates, 80 halftones, 4 maps. vi + 320pp. 6⅛ x 9⅛. 22366-3 Paperbound $5.00

Ten Books on Architecture, Vitruvius. By any standards the most important book on architecture ever written. Early Roman discussion of aesthetics of building, construction methods, orders, sites, and every other aspect of architecture has inspired, instructed architecture for about 2,000 years. Stands behind Palladio, Michelangelo, Bramante, Wren, countless others. Definitive Morris H. Morgan translation. 68 illustrations. xii + 331pp. 20645-9 Paperbound $3.00

The Four Books of Architecture, Andrea Palladio. Translated into every major Western European language in the two centuries following its publication in 1570, this has been one of the most influential books in the history of architecture. Complete reprint of the 1738 Isaac Ware edition. New introduction by Adolf Placzek, Columbia Univ. 216 plates. xxii + 110pp. of text. 9½ x 12¾. 21308-0 Clothbound $12.50

Sticks and Stones: A Study of American Architecture and Civilization, Lewis Mumford.One of the great classics of American cultural history. American architecture from the medieval-inspired earliest forms to the early 20th century; evolution of structure and style, and reciprocal influences on environment. 21 photographic illustrations. 238pp. 20202-X Paperbound $2.00

The American Builder's Companion, Asher Benjamin. The most widely used early 19th century architectural style and source book, for colonial up into Greek Revival periods. Extensive development of geometry of carpentering, construction of sashes, frames, doors, stairs; plans and elevations of domestic and other buildings. Hundreds of thousands of houses were built according to this book, now invaluable to historians, architects, restorers, etc. 1827 edition. 59 plates. 114pp. 7⅞ x 10¾. 22236-5 Paperbound $3.50

Dutch Houses in the Hudson Valley Before 1776, Helen Wilkinson Reynolds. The standard survey of the Dutch colonial house and outbuildings, with constructional features, decoration, and local history associated with individual homesteads. Introduction by Franklin D. Roosevelt. Map. 150 illustrations. 469pp. 6⅝ x 9¼. 21469-9 Paperbound $5.00

THE ARCHITECTURE OF COUNTRY HOUSES, Andrew J. Downing. Together with Vaux's *Villas and Cottages* this is the basic book for Hudson River Gothic architecture of the middle Victorian period. Full, sound discussions of general aspects of housing, architecture, style, decoration, furnishing, together with scores of detailed house plans, illustrations of specific buildings, accompanied by full text. Perhaps the most influential single American architectural book. 1850 edition. Introduction by J. Stewart Johnson. 321 figures, 34 architectural designs. xvi + 560pp.
22003-6 Paperbound $4.00

LOST EXAMPLES OF COLONIAL ARCHITECTURE, John Mead Howells. Full-page photographs of buildings that have disappeared or been so altered as to be denatured, including many designed by major early American architects. 245 plates. xvii + 248pp. 7⅞ x 10¾.
21143-6 Paperbound $3.50

DOMESTIC ARCHITECTURE OF THE AMERICAN COLONIES AND OF THE EARLY REPUBLIC, Fiske Kimball. Foremost architect and restorer of Williamsburg and Monticello covers nearly 200 homes between 1620-1825. Architectural details, construction, style features, special fixtures, floor plans, etc. Generally considered finest work in its area. 219 illustrations of houses, doorways, windows, capital mantels. xx + 314pp. 7⅞ x 10¾.
21743-4 Paperbound $4.00

EARLY AMERICAN ROOMS: 1650-1858, edited by Russell Hawes Kettell. Tour of 12 rooms, each representative of a different era in American history and each furnished, decorated, designed and occupied in the style of the era. 72 plans and elevations, 8-page color section, etc., show fabrics, wall papers, arrangements, etc. Full descriptive text. xvii + 200pp. of text. 8⅜ x 11¼.
21633-0 Paperbound $5.00

THE FITZWILLIAM VIRGINAL BOOK, edited by J. Fuller Maitland and W. B. Squire. Full modern printing of famous early 17th-century ms. volume of 300 works by Morley, Byrd, Bull, Gibbons, etc. For piano or other modern keyboard instrument; easy to read format. xxxvi + 938pp. 8⅜ x 11.
21068-5, 21069-3 Two volumes, Paperbound $10.00

KEYBOARD MUSIC, Johann Sebastian Bach. Bach Gesellschaft edition. A rich selection of Bach's masterpieces for the harpsichord: the six English Suites, six French Suites, the six Partitas (Clavierübung part I), the Goldberg Variations (Clavierübung part IV), the fifteen Two-Part Inventions and the fifteen Three-Part Sinfonias. Clearly reproduced on large sheets with ample margins; eminently playable. vi + 312pp. 8⅛ x 11.
22360-4 Paperbound $5.00

THE MUSIC OF BACH: AN INTRODUCTION, Charles Sanford Terry. A fine, non-technical introduction to Bach's music, both instrumental and vocal. Covers organ music, chamber music, passion music, other types. Analyzes themes, developments, innovations. x + 114pp.
21075-8 Paperbound $1.50

BEETHOVEN AND HIS NINE SYMPHONIES, Sir George Grove. Noted British musicologist provides best history, analysis, commentary on symphonies. Very thorough, rigorously accurate; necessary to both advanced student and amateur music lover. 436 musical passages. vii + 407 pp.
20334-4 Paperbound $2.75

JOHANN SEBASTIAN BACH, Philipp Spitta. One of the great classics of musicology, this definitive analysis of Bach's music (and life) has never been surpassed. Lucid, nontechnical analyses of hundreds of pieces (30 pages devoted to St. Matthew Passion, 26 to B Minor Mass). Also includes major analysis of 18th-century music. 450 musical examples. 40-page musical supplement. Total of xx + 1799pp.

(EUK) 22278-0, 22279-9 Two volumes, Clothbound $17.50

MOZART AND HIS PIANO CONCERTOS, Cuthbert Girdlestone. The only full-length study of an important area of Mozart's creativity. Provides detailed analyses of all 23 concertos, traces inspirational sources. 417 musical examples. Second edition. 509pp.

21271-8 Paperbound $3.50

THE PERFECT WAGNERITE: A COMMENTARY ON THE NIBLUNG'S RING, George Bernard Shaw. Brilliant and still relevant criticism in remarkable essays on Wagner's Ring cycle, Shaw's ideas on political and social ideology behind the plots, role of Leitmotifs, vocal requisites, etc. Prefaces. xxi + 136pp.

(USO) 21707-8 Paperbound $1.75

DON GIOVANNI, W. A. Mozart. Complete libretto, modern English translation; biographies of composer and librettist; accounts of early performances and critical reaction. Lavishly illustrated. All the material you need to understand and appreciate this great work. Dover Opera Guide and Libretto Series; translated and introduced by Ellen Bleiler. 92 illustrations. 209pp.

21134-7 Paperbound $2.00

BASIC ELECTRICITY, U. S. Bureau of Naval Personel. Originally a training course, best non-technical coverage of basic theory of electricity and its applications. Fundamental concepts, batteries, circuits, conductors and wiring techniques, AC and DC, inductance and capacitance, generators, motors, transformers, magnetic amplifiers, synchros, servomechanisms, etc. Also covers blue-prints, electrical diagrams, etc. Many questions, with answers. 349 illustrations. x + 448pp. 6½ x 9¼.

20973-3 Paperbound $3.50

REPRODUCTION OF SOUND, Edgar Villchur. Thorough coverage for laymen of high fidelity systems, reproducing systems in general, needles, amplifiers, preamps, loudspeakers, feedback, explaining physical background. "A rare talent for making technicalities vividly comprehensible," R. Darrell, *High Fidelity*. 69 figures. iv + 92pp.

21515-6 Paperbound $1.35

HEAR ME TALKIN' TO YA: THE STORY OF JAZZ AS TOLD BY THE MEN WHO MADE IT, Nat Shapiro and Nat Hentoff. Louis Armstrong, Fats Waller, Jo Jones, Clarence Williams, Billy Holiday, Duke Ellington, Jelly Roll Morton and dozens of other jazz greats tell how it was in Chicago's South Side, New Orleans, depression Harlem and the modern West Coast as jazz was born and grew. xvi + 429pp.

21726-4 Paperbound $3.00

FABLES OF AESOP, translated by Sir Roger L'Estrange. A reproduction of the very rare 1931 Paris edition; a selection of the most interesting fables, together with 50 imaginative drawings by Alexander Calder. v + 128pp. 6½x9¼.

21780-9 Paperbound $1.50

AGAINST THE GRAIN (A REBOURS), Joris K. Huysmans. Filled with weird images, evidences of a bizarre imagination, exotic experiments with hallucinatory drugs, rich tastes and smells and the diversions of its sybarite hero Duc Jean des Esseintes, this classic novel pushed 19th-century literary decadence to its limits. Full unabridged edition. Do not confuse this with abridged editions generally sold. Introduction by Havelock Ellis. xlix + 206pp. 22190-3 Paperbound $2.50

VARIORUM SHAKESPEARE: HAMLET. Edited by Horace H. Furness; a landmark of American scholarship. Exhaustive footnotes and appendices treat all doubtful words and phrases, as well as suggested critical emendations throughout the play's history. First volume contains editor's own text, collated with all Quartos and Folios. Second volume contains full first Quarto, translations of Shakespeare's sources (Belleforest, and Saxo Grammaticus), Der Bestrafte Brudermord, and many essays on critical and historical points of interest by major authorities of past and present. Includes details of staging and costuming over the years. By far the best edition available for serious students of Shakespeare. Total of xx + 905pp. 21004-9, 21005-7, 2 volumes, Paperbound $7.00

A LIFE OF WILLIAM SHAKESPEARE, Sir Sidney Lee. This is the standard life of Shakespeare, summarizing everything known about Shakespeare and his plays. Incredibly rich in material, broad in coverage, clear and judicious, it has served thousands as the best introduction to Shakespeare. 1931 edition. 9 plates. xxix + 792pp. 21967-4 Paperbound $3.75

MASTERS OF THE DRAMA, John Gassner. Most comprehensive history of the drama in print, covering every tradition from Greeks to modern Europe and America, including India, Far East, etc. Covers more than 800 dramatists, 2000 plays, with biographical material, plot summaries, theatre history, criticism, etc. "Best of its kind in English," *New Republic*. 77 illustrations. xxii + 890pp. 20100-7 Clothbound $10.00

THE EVOLUTION OF THE ENGLISH LANGUAGE, George McKnight. The growth of English, from the 14th century to the present. Unusual, non-technical account presents basic information in very interesting form: sound shifts, change in grammar and syntax, vocabulary growth, similar topics. Abundantly illustrated with quotations. Formerly *Modern English in the Making*. xii + 590pp. 21932-1 Paperbound $3.50

AN ETYMOLOGICAL DICTIONARY OF MODERN ENGLISH, Ernest Weekley. Fullest, richest work of its sort, by foremost British lexicographer. Detailed word histories, including many colloquial and archaic words; extensive quotations. Do not confuse this with the Concise Etymological Dictionary, which is much abridged. Total of xxvii + 830pp. 6½ x 9¼. 21873-2, 21874-0 Two volumes, Paperbound $7.90

FLATLAND: A ROMANCE OF MANY DIMENSIONS, E. A. Abbott. Classic of science-fiction explores ramifications of life in a two-dimensional world, and what happens when a three-dimensional being intrudes. Amusing reading, but also useful as introduction to thought about hyperspace. Introduction by Banesh Hoffmann. 16 illustrations. xx + 103pp. 20001-9 Paperbound $1.00

POEMS OF ANNE BRADSTREET, edited with an introduction by Robert Hutchinson. A new selection of poems by America's first poet and perhaps the first significant woman poet in the English language. 48 poems display her development in works of considerable variety—love poems, domestic poems, religious meditations, formal elegies, "quaternions," etc. Notes, bibliography. viii + 222pp.
22160-1 Paperbound $2.50

THREE GOTHIC NOVELS: THE CASTLE OF OTRANTO BY HORACE WALPOLE; VATHEK BY WILLIAM BECKFORD; THE VAMPYRE BY JOHN POLIDORI, WITH FRAGMENT OF A NOVEL BY LORD BYRON, edited by E. F. Bleiler. The first Gothic novel, by Walpole; the finest Oriental tale in English, by Beckford; powerful Romantic supernatural story in versions by Polidori and Byron. All extremely important in history of literature; all still exciting, packed with supernatural thrills, ghosts, haunted castles, magic, etc. xl + 291pp.
21232-7 Paperbound $2.50

THE BEST TALES OF HOFFMANN, E. T. A. Hoffmann. 10 of Hoffmann's most important stories, in modern re-editings of standard translations: Nutcracker and the King of Mice, Signor Formica, Automata, The Sandman, Rath Krespel, The Golden Flowerpot, Master Martin the Cooper, The Mines of Falun, The King's Betrothed, A New Year's Eve Adventure. 7 illustrations by Hoffmann. Edited by E. F. Bleiler. xxxix + 419pp.
21793-0 Paperbound $3.00

GHOST AND HORROR STORIES OF AMBROSE BIERCE, Ambrose Bierce. 23 strikingly modern stories of the horrors latent in the human mind: The Eyes of the Panther, The Damned Thing, An Occurrence at Owl Creek Bridge, An Inhabitant of Carcosa, etc., plus the dream-essay, Visions of the Night. Edited by E. F. Bleiler. xxii + 199pp.
20767-6 Paperbound $1.50

BEST GHOST STORIES OF J. S. LEFANU, J. Sheridan LeFanu. Finest stories by Victorian master often considered greatest supernatural writer of all. Carmilla, Green Tea, The Haunted Baronet, The Familiar, and 12 others. Most never before available in the U. S. A. Edited by E. F. Bleiler. 8 illustrations from Victorian publications. xvii + 467pp.
20415-4 Paperbound $3.00

MATHEMATICAL FOUNDATIONS OF INFORMATION THEORY, A. I. Khinchin. Comprehensive introduction to work of Shannon, McMillan, Feinstein and Khinchin, placing these investigations on a rigorous mathematical basis. Covers entropy concept in probability theory, uniqueness theorem, Shannon's inequality, ergodic sources, the E property, martingale concept, noise, Feinstein's fundamental lemma, Shanon's first and second theorems. Translated by R. A. Silverman and M. D. Friedman. iii + 120pp.
60434-9 Paperbound $2.00

SEVEN SCIENCE FICTION NOVELS, H. G. Wells. The standard collection of the great novels. Complete, unabridged. *First Men in the Moon, Island of Dr. Moreau, War of the Worlds, Food of the Gods, Invisible Man, Time Machine, In the Days of the Comet.* Not only science fiction fans, but every educated person owes it to himself to read these novels. 1015pp. (USO) 20264-X Clothbound $6.00

LAST AND FIRST MEN AND STAR MAKER, TWO SCIENCE FICTION NOVELS, Olaf Stapledon. Greatest future histories in science fiction. In the first, human intelligence is the "hero," through strange paths of evolution, interplanetary invasions, incredible technologies, near extinctions and reemergences. Star Maker describes the quest of a band of star rovers for intelligence itself, through time and space: weird inhuman civilizations, crustacean minds, symbiotic worlds, etc. Complete, unabridged. v + 438pp.   (USO) 21962-3 Paperbound $2.50

THREE PROPHETIC NOVELS, H. G. WELLS. Stages of a consistently planned future for mankind. *When the Sleeper Wakes*, and *A Story of the Days to Come*, anticipate *Brave New World* and *1984*, in the 21st Century; *The Time Machine*, only complete version in print, shows farther future and the end of mankind. All show Wells's greatest gifts as storyteller and novelist. Edited by E. F. Bleiler. x + 335pp.   (USO) 20605-X Paperbound $2.50

THE DEVIL'S DICTIONARY, Ambrose Bierce. America's own Oscar Wilde—Ambrose Bierce—offers his barbed iconoclastic wisdom in over 1,000 definitions hailed by H. L. Mencken as "some of the most gorgeous witticisms in the English language." 145pp.   20487-1 Paperbound $1.25

MAX AND MORITZ, Wilhelm Busch. Great children's classic, father of comic strip, of two bad boys, Max and Moritz. Also Ker and Plunk (Plisch und Plumm), Cat and Mouse, Deceitful Henry, Ice-Peter, The Boy and the Pipe, and five other pieces. Original German, with English translation. Edited by H. Arthur Klein; translations by various hands and H. Arthur Klein. vi + 216pp.   20181-3 Paperbound $2.00

PIGS IS PIGS AND OTHER FAVORITES, Ellis Parker Butler. The title story is one of the best humor short stories, as Mike Flannery obfuscates biology and English. Also included, That Pup of Murchison's, The Great American Pie Company, and Perkins of Portland. 14 illustrations. v + 109pp.   21532-6 Paperbound $1.25

THE PETERKIN PAPERS, Lucretia P. Hale. It takes genius to be as stupidly mad as the Peterkins, as they decide to become wise, celebrate the "Fourth," keep a cow, and otherwise strain the resources of the Lady from Philadelphia. Basic book of American humor. 153 illustrations. 219pp.   20794-3 Paperbound $2.00

PERRAULT'S FAIRY TALES, translated by A. E. Johnson and S. R. Littlewood, with 34 full-page illustrations by Gustave Doré. All the original Perrault stories—Cinderella, Sleeping Beauty, Bluebeard, Little Red Riding Hood, Puss in Boots, Tom Thumb, etc.—with their witty verse morals and the magnificent illustrations of Doré. One of the five or six great books of European fairy tales. viii + 117pp. 8⅛ x 11.   22311-6 Paperbound $2.00

OLD HUNGARIAN FAIRY TALES, Baroness Orczy. Favorites translated and adapted by author of the *Scarlet Pimpernel*. Eight fairy tales include "The Suitors of Princess Fire-Fly," "The Twin Hunchbacks," "Mr. Cuttlefish's Love Story," and "The Enchanted Cat." This little volume of magic and adventure will captivate children as it has for generations. 90 drawings by Montagu Barstow. 96pp.   (USO) 22293-4 Paperbound $1.95

THE RED FAIRY BOOK, Andrew Lang. Lang's color fairy books have long been children's favorites. This volume includes Rapunzel, Jack and the Bean-stalk and 35 other stories, familiar and unfamiliar. 4 plates, 93 illustrations x + 367pp.
21673-X Paperbound $2.50

THE BLUE FAIRY BOOK, Andrew Lang. Lang's tales come from all countries and all times. Here are 37 tales from Grimm, the Arabian Nights, Greek Mythology, and other fascinating sources. 8 plates, 130 illustrations. xi + 390pp.
21437-0 Paperbound $2.50

HOUSEHOLD STORIES BY THE BROTHERS GRIMM. Classic English-language edition of the well-known tales — Rumpelstiltskin, Snow White, Hansel and Gretel, The Twelve Brothers, Faithful John, Rapunzel, Tom Thumb (52 stories in all). Translated into simple, straightforward English by Lucy Crane. Ornamented with headpieces, vignettes, elaborate decorative initials and a dozen full-page illustrations by Walter Crane. x + 269pp.
21080-4 Paperbound **$2.00**

THE MERRY ADVENTURES OF ROBIN HOOD, Howard Pyle. The finest modern versions of the traditional ballads and tales about the great English outlaw. Howard Pyle's complete prose version, with every word, every illustration of the first edition. Do not confuse this facsimile of the original (1883) with modern editions that change text or illustrations. 23 plates plus many page decorations. xxii + 296pp.
22043-5 Paperbound $2.50

THE STORY OF KING ARTHUR AND HIS KNIGHTS, Howard Pyle. The finest children's version of the life of King Arthur; brilliantly retold by Pyle, with 48 of his most imaginative illustrations. xviii + 313pp. 6⅛ x 9¼.
21445-1 Paperbound $2.50

THE WONDERFUL WIZARD OF OZ, L. Frank Baum. America's finest children's book in facsimile of first edition with all Denslow illustrations in full color. The edition a child should have. Introduction by Martin Gardner. 23 color plates, scores of drawings. iv + 267pp.
20691-2 Paperbound $2.50

THE MARVELOUS LAND OF OZ, L. Frank Baum. The second Oz book, every bit as imaginative as the Wizard. The hero is a boy named Tip, but the Scarecrow and the Tin Woodman are back, as is the Oz magic. 16 color plates, 120 drawings by John R. Neill. 287pp.
20692-0 Paperbound $2.50

THE MAGICAL MONARCH OF MO, L. Frank Baum. Remarkable adventures in a land even stranger than Oz. The best of Baum's books not in the Oz series. 15 color plates and dozens of drawings by Frank Verbeck. xviii + 237pp.
21892-9 Paperbound $2.25

THE BAD CHILD'S BOOK OF BEASTS, MORE BEASTS FOR WORSE CHILDREN, A MORAL ALPHABET, Hilaire Belloc. Three complete humor classics in one volume. Be kind to the frog, and do not call him names . . . and 28 other whimsical animals. Familiar favorites and some not so well known. Illustrated by Basil Blackwell. 156pp.
(USO) 20749-8 Paperbound $1.50

EAST O' THE SUN AND WEST O' THE MOON, George W. Dasent. Considered the best of all translations of these Norwegian folk tales, this collection has been enjoyed by generations of children (and folklorists too). Includes True and Untrue, Why the Sea is Salt, East O' the Sun and West O' the Moon, Why the Bear is Stumpy-Tailed, Boots and the Troll, The Cock and the Hen, Rich Peter the Pedlar, and 52 more. The only edition with all 59 tales. 77 illustrations by Erik Werenskiold and Theodor Kittelsen. xv + 418pp.          22521-6 Paperbound $3.50

GOOPS AND HOW TO BE THEM, Gelett Burgess. Classic of tongue-in-cheek humor, masquerading as etiquette book. 87 verses, twice as many cartoons, show mischievous Goops as they demonstrate to children virtues of table manners, neatness, courtesy, etc. Favorite for generations. viii + 88pp. $6\frac{1}{2}$ x $9\frac{1}{4}$.
          22233-0 Paperbound $1.25

ALICE'S ADVENTURES UNDER GROUND, Lewis Carroll. The first version, quite different from the final Alice in Wonderland, printed out by Carroll himself with his own illustrations. Complete facsimile of the "million dollar" manuscript Carroll gave to Alice Liddell in 1864. Introduction by Martin Gardner. viii + 96pp. Title and dedication pages in color.          21482-6 Paperbound $1.25

THE BROWNIES, THEIR BOOK, Palmer Cox. Small as mice, cunning as foxes, exuberant and full of mischief, the Brownies go to the zoo, toy shop, seashore, circus, etc., in 24 verse adventures and 266 illustrations. Long a favorite, since their first appearance in St. Nicholas Magazine. xi + 144pp. $6\frac{5}{8}$ x $9\frac{1}{4}$.
          21265-3 Paperbound $1.75

SONGS OF CHILDHOOD, Walter De La Mare. Published (under the pseudonym Walter Ramal) when De La Mare was only 29, this charming collection has long been a favorite children's book. A facsimile of the first edition in paper, the 47 poems capture the simplicity of the nursery rhyme and the ballad, including such lyrics as I Met Eve, Tartary, The Silver Penny. vii + 106pp. (USO) 21972-0 Paperbound
          $1.25

THE COMPLETE NONSENSE OF EDWARD LEAR, Edward Lear. The finest 19th-century humorist-cartoonist in full: all nonsense limericks, zany alphabets, Owl and Pussycat, songs, nonsense botany, and more than 500 illustrations by Lear himself. Edited by Holbrook Jackson. xxix + 287pp.          (USO) 20167-8 Paperbound $2.00

BILLY WHISKERS: THE AUTOBIOGRAPHY OF A GOAT, Frances Trego Montgomery. A favorite of children since the early 20th century, here are the escapades of that rambunctious, irresistible and mischievous goat—Billy Whiskers. Much in the spirit of Peck's Bad Boy, this is a book that children never tire of reading or hearing. All the original familiar illustrations by W. H. Fry are included: 6 color plates, 18 black and white drawings. 159pp.          22345-0 Paperbound $2.00

MOTHER GOOSE MELODIES. Faithful republication of the fabulously rare Munroe and Francis "copyright 1833" Boston edition—the most important Mother Goose collection, usually referred to as the "original." Familiar rhymes plus many rare ones, with wonderful old woodcut illustrations. Edited by E. F. Bleiler. 128pp. $4\frac{1}{2}$ x $6\frac{3}{8}$.          22577-1 Paperbound $1.00

TWO LITTLE SAVAGES; BEING THE ADVENTURES OF TWO BOYS WHO LIVED AS INDIANS AND WHAT THEY LEARNED, Ernest Thompson Seton. Great classic of nature and boyhood provides a vast range of woodlore in most palatable form, a genuinely entertaining story. Two farm boys build a teepee in woods and live in it for a month, working out Indian solutions to living problems, star lore, birds and animals, plants, etc. 293 illustrations. vii + 286pp.

20985-7 Paperbound $2.50

PETER PIPER'S PRACTICAL PRINCIPLES OF PLAIN & PERFECT PRONUNCIATION. Alliterative jingles and tongue-twisters of surprising charm, that made their first appearance in America about 1830. Republished in full with the spirited woodcut illustrations from this earliest American edition. 32pp. 4½ x 6⅜.

22560-7 Paperbound $1.00

SCIENCE EXPERIMENTS AND AMUSEMENTS FOR CHILDREN, Charles Vivian. 73 easy experiments, requiring only materials found at home or easily available, such as candles, coins, steel wool, etc.; illustrate basic phenomena like vacuum, simple chemical reaction, etc. All safe. Modern, well-planned. Formerly *Science Games for Children*. 102 photos, numerous drawings. 96pp. 6⅛ x 9¼.

21856-2 Paperbound $1.25

AN INTRODUCTION TO CHESS MOVES AND TACTICS SIMPLY EXPLAINED, Leonard Barden. Informal intermediate introduction, quite strong in explaining reasons for moves. Covers basic material, tactics, important openings, traps, positional play in middle game, end game. Attempts to isolate patterns and recurrent configurations. Formerly *Chess*. 58 figures. 102pp. (USO) 21210-6 Paperbound $1.25

LASKER'S MANUAL OF CHESS, Dr. Emanuel Lasker. Lasker was not only one of the five great World Champions, he was also one of the ablest expositors, theorists, and analysts. In many ways, his Manual, permeated with his philosophy of battle, filled with keen insights, is one of the greatest works ever written on chess. Filled with analyzed games by the great players. A single-volume library that will profit almost any chess player, beginner or master. 308 diagrams. xli X 349pp.

20640-8 Paperbound $2.75

THE MASTER BOOK OF MATHEMATICAL RECREATIONS, Fred Schuh. In opinion of many the finest work ever prepared on mathematical puzzles, stunts, recreations; exhaustively thorough explanations of mathematics involved, analysis of effects, citation of puzzles and games. Mathematics involved is elementary. Translated by F. Göbel. 194 figures. xxiv + 430pp.

22134-2 Paperbound $3.50

MATHEMATICS, MAGIC AND MYSTERY, Martin Gardner. Puzzle editor for Scientific American explains mathematics behind various mystifying tricks: card tricks, stage "mind reading," coin and match tricks, counting out games, geometric dissections, etc. Probability sets, theory of numbers clearly explained. Also provides more than 400 tricks, guaranteed to work, that you can do. 135 illustrations. xii + 176pp.

20335-2 Paperbound $1.75

MATHEMATICAL PUZZLES FOR BEGINNERS AND ENTHUSIASTS, Geoffrey Mott-Smith. 189 puzzles from easy to difficult—involving arithmetic, logic, algebra, properties of digits, probability, etc.—for enjoyment and mental stimulus. Explanation of mathematical principles behind the puzzles. 135 illustrations. viii + 248pp.
20198-8 Paperbound $1.75

PAPER FOLDING FOR BEGINNERS, William D. Murray and Francis J. Rigney. Easiest book on the market, clearest instructions on making interesting, beautiful origami. Sail boats, cups, roosters, frogs that move legs, bonbon boxes, standing birds, etc. 40 projects; more than 275 diagrams and photographs. 94pp.
20713-7 Paperbound $1.00

TRICKS AND GAMES ON THE POOL TABLE, Fred Herrmann. 79 tricks and games—some solitaires, some for two or more players, some competitive games—to entertain you between formal games. Mystifying shots and throws, unusual caroms, tricks involving such props as cork, coins, a hat, etc. Formerly *Fun on the Pool Table*. 77 figures. 95pp.
21814-7 Paperbound $1.25

HAND SHADOWS TO BE THROWN UPON THE WALL: A SERIES OF NOVEL AND AMUSING FIGURES FORMED BY THE HAND, Henry Bursill. Delightful picturebook from great-grandfather's day shows how to make 18 different hand shadows: a bird that flies, duck that quacks, dog that wags his tail, camel, goose, deer, boy, turtle, etc. Only book of its sort. vi + 33pp. 6½ x 9¼. 21779-5 Paperbound $1.00

WHITTLING AND WOODCARVING, E. J. Tangerman. 18th printing of best book on market. "If you can cut a potato you can carve" toys and puzzles, chains, chessmen, caricatures, masks, frames, woodcut blocks, surface patterns, much more. Information on tools, woods, techniques. Also goes into serious wood sculpture from Middle Ages to present, East and West. 464 photos, figures. x + 293pp.
20965-2 Paperbound $2.00

HISTORY OF PHILOSOPHY, Julián Marías. Possibly the clearest, most easily followed, best planned, most useful one-volume history of philosophy on the market; neither skimpy nor overfull. Full details on system of every major philosopher and dozens of less important thinkers from pre-Socratics up to Existentialism and later. Strong on many European figures usually omitted. Has gone through dozens of editions in Europe. 1966 edition, translated by Stanley Appelbaum and Clarence Strowbridge. xviii + 505pp. 21739-6 Paperbound $3.50

YOGA: A SCIENTIFIC EVALUATION, Kovoor T. Behanan. Scientific but non-technical study of physiological results of yoga exercises; done under auspices of Yale U. Relations to Indian thought, to psychoanalysis, etc. 16 photos. xxiii + 270pp.
20505-3 Paperbound $2.50

*Prices subject to change without notice.*
Available at your book dealer or write for free catalogue to Dept. GI, Dover Publications, Inc., 180 Varick St., N. Y., N. Y. 10014. Dover publishes more than 150 books each year on science, elementary and advanced mathematics, biology, music, art, literary history, social sciences and other areas.